52 Ideas for Infant Assemblies Plus 52 Brand New Songs

CHRIS CHESTERTON
AND
ELAINE BUCKLEY

MONARCH
BOOKS

First published by Monarch Books 1999

ISBN 1 85424 433 7

Editorial office: Monarch Books, Broadway House, The Broadway, Crowborough, East Sussex TN6 1HQ

British Library Cataloguing Data
A catalogue record for this book is available from the British Library.

Illustrations by James Walton

Designed and produced for the publisher by
Bookprint Creative Services
PO Box 827, BN21 3YJ, England
Printed in Great Britain.

CONTENTS

FOREWORD

Having worked for thirty years in early years education, I know only too well how difficult it is to find ways into dealing with things moral and spiritual with young children. Yet they are invariably open and ready to learn when the assembly is focused and the focus is right. There are some people who have a clear gift for communicating with children and whose faith and talent translates itself into real lessons for real life. Chris Chesterton and Elaine Buckley are two such people. This book is a combination of Elaine's lively and child-centred songs with Chris's relevant and 'hands-on' approach to Bible stories and the moral issues they raise.

This collection somehow circumvents the misunderstandings and prejudices which adults often develop about God. Instead it draws on the openness and expectancy which characterise a young child's attitude. I have been privileged to see Chris in action many times and have found his approach and material a great blessing. Having also been fortunate enough to have Elaine try out her songs with my children at school I know how much pleasure they give to children (and teachers!). The songs make truth accessible. They are catchy, easy to learn and are frequently sung round school by children at the sand tray and water bath just for the fun of it.

This book is an important resource for teachers of young children. While there have been many which meet the needs of Key Stage 2, teachers in the early years have been waiting for a book which is tailor made for infants. The wait is over — this is it. I believe you will soon find yourself being as grateful as I am for all that it contains.

Susan Aldridge
Headteacher and author of *Who is this Jesus?* the musical.

INTRODUCTION

This book is all about exploring. It is about helping young children to explore the world they live in, the world of sounds and shapes and smells and the growing awareness of their own bodies. It is about exploring the invisible world of feelings and love and relationships, and the world of the spirit, so hard to define and yet so important. It is about exploring timeless stories from the Bible and finding how they relate to those other external and internal worlds of today's child.

We have endeavoured to root these assemblies firmly within the ethos and broad curriculum outlines of the Key Stage 1 school. Yet school worship can also be a precious breathing space in a crowded day when wider horizons can be glimpsed. We have tried to open up some of those horizons.

Because creating these songs and stories has been an exploration for us too, we hope you and the children will find here the same freshness and enjoyment we have found in writing and using them.

USING THIS BOOK

Where **RESOURCES** are needed for a talk, they have mainly been kept simple and easy to find, either at home or in school. A photocopiable section at the back of the book contains a small number of pictures for use with some of the assemblies.

The **GUIDE LETTERS** at the head of the talks are intended to provide instant information for suggested use. They are as follows:

C — suitable for a classroom assembly.

P — suitable for a class to prepare to present to the rest of the school. Brackets indicate that this is optional.

M — song which also works well as part of a musical movement lesson.

T — song with a traditional tune (and therefore easily useable by anyone who does not read music).

S — song which we have found works particularly well with Special Needs pupils.

A — song with accompanying actions

ADDITIONAL MUSIC RESOURCE

A number of the songs in this book feature in Elaine Buckley's recording *A Basketful of Rhyme*.

This is a unique collection of easy-to-learn action songs for babies and young children. It is a great resource for non-musical leaders or teachers and can be most helpful for the nursery class participating in an assembly. Many of the songs have also been used with children with learning difficulties.

Songs from this book featured on the recording are: Flap Your Wings; Gimme Five; God Gave Noah a Job To Do; Have You Ever Tried Reaching for the Sky?; I Am a Robot; I Know the Story of a Special Baby; I'm Not an Accident; Incy Wincy Spider; Jesus and God Go Together; Nod Your Head If You've Got a Bed; Show Your Love; Thank You, God, You're Fantastic; There's More Than Me; plus thirteen others.

A Basketful of Rhyme is available on CD or cassette from bookshops or direct from Elaine Buckley at: 5 Marshall Road, Mapperley, Nottingham NG3 6HS.

APPLES AND PEARS FOR US TO SHARE

Appreciating the abundance around us and the wonder of how so great a variety is made of such simple 'ingredients'. Suitable for a Harvest service.

RESOURCES

- Pictures of food, or art materials, or Harvest items.
- A mixing bowl, a wooden spoon, a drinking-straw, soil and water.

CLASS PREPARATION (Optional)

- Children cut and mount or paint or choose a favourite food item each. Talk about their choices and why they like those foods. (Vocabulary and concepts: tastes, colours, textures, personal preferences.)

ASSEMBLY

- If a class has prepared them, children can show their choices. 'My favourite food is.... ', adding 'I like it because.... ' if they are able. Alternatively, ask some children to talk about their favourite food.
- Tell the children you have a recipe for making one of their favourite foods, a fruit (banana or peach or whatever a child has mentioned). Ask a child to help you make the fruit using your recipe. Get out the mixing bowl and give her the spoon.

  Produce the first ingredient: soil. Pour it in the bowl. Ask the child if she is looking forward to the food you are going to make!

  Produce the next ingredient: water. Pour it in the bowl and get the child to stir it into runny mud. Keep telling her you are sure she is going to enjoy what you are making!

  The third ingredient is sunlight. If the sun isn't shining, hold the bowl up to a light instead.

  For the last ingredient, give the child the straw and ask her to blow bubbles in the mud. Air is a very important ingredient in the recipe.

Does she want to eat it now? Does anybody? No! But bananas and peaches and all other fruit really are made from these ingredients. Hidden away inside it, each fruit tree has its own secret recipe for turning soil and water and sunlight and air into delicious fruit. Every plant that grows, all the bits of plants we eat — peas and beans and lettuce leaves and tomatoes — are all made from the same ingredients. Aren't they clever! Or perhaps the really clever one is God who made the whole world and all the plants in the first place.

And the meat we eat comes from animals that eat plants. Cows eat grass and chickens eat corn. So in the end, *all* the food we eat comes from the same ingredients.

- A sketch of the 'recipe' with the 'ingredients' labelled (soil, rain, sunshine, air) could be shown to reinforce the factual side of the message.
- Sing the song. The chorus is a prayer.

BIBLE BACKGROUND

You make the grass for cattle and vegetables for the use of man.
You make food grow from the earth.

Psalm 104:14

APPLES AND PEARS
With bounce
C F G C
Apples and pears for us to share.
Crackers and cheese to eat when you please.
Chocolate and sweets for spe- cial treats.
C F G C C F
Pea- ches and plums to fill our tums. Bis- cuits and cake,
But- ter and bread keeps us well fed. Ban- gers and mash,
Chips with fish is very tasty dish. Bananas and rice
G C F G C
piz- za and steak, I'm in the mood for food.
corned beef hash,
grapes are very nice,
Chorus
C F G C F G
Thank you God for the sun and the rain. Making things grow a-gain
C F G C
and a- gain. Thank you God for the sun and the rain.
F G7
Making things grow a- gain and a- gain and a- gain and a-gain and a- gain
C

AS HIGH AS THE HEAVENS ABOVE

Considering contrasts leads into thoughts about different kinds of love.

RESOURCES

- Pairs of contrasting items to see or feel or hear.

ASSEMBLY

- Sing the song. At the end of the line, 'As deep as the breath we take', everybody takes a deep breath and holds it for a moment before going on. Children love this.
- Lead the children in experimenting with some contrasts in breathing: deep and shallow, quick and slow, quiet and noisy.
- Use objects and sounds and the children themselves to think about contrasts, eg firm/soft, loud/quiet, smooth/rough, heavy/light, big/small, tall/short, broad/narrow, hot/cold, etc.
- In the song we sing about Jesus' love for us. Jesus' love is like parents' love or teachers' love: sometimes it can be gentle and sometimes it can be tough; sometimes it can be firm and sometimes encouraging.

  One day some mothers brought their babies to Jesus. Jesus' friends knew he was very tired, so they told the mothers to go away. But Jesus told them to bring the babies and toddlers. He took them on his knee and blessed them. That was soft and gentle love.

  At Easter time Jesus let the soldiers arrest him and kill him on a cross. He did that to show how much God loves people and wants to save them. That was tough love.

  Sometimes Jesus' friends quarrelled and said silly things. Jesus told them off. He still loved them, but he wanted them to stop being silly. That was firm love.

  One day Jesus sent his friends off to tell lots of other people about him. When they came back he told them what a good job they had done and how pleased he was. That was encouraging love.

  So love can be all sorts of different things at the same time, but it's still love. Just like breathing can be deep or shallow, slow or quick, quiet or noisy.

- **A Prayer**

  Father God, thank you for the love of our parents. Thank you for the love of grandparents and other members of our families. Thank you for the love of our teachers and friends. Thank you for the love of Jesus. Thank you for all the different kinds of love there are in the world. Amen.

- Sing the song again.

BIBLE BACKGROUND

Jesus... was displeased. He said to them, 'Let the little children come to me.'

Mark 10:14

AS HIGH AS THE HEAVENS ABOVE

BEARS WITH CLAWS AND LIONS WITH ROARS

Appreciating some of the wonders of the animal world.

RESOURCES

- Pictures of a snail and a thrush, if available. A sound-effects tape with the song of a thrush (or another songbird) is a very effective extra.

CLASS PREPARATION

- Work with a group of children on suitable actions and body movements for each animal in the song. Children might also produce their own rhyming pairs as in the song. Good for language development, body awareness and use of imagination.

  Another possibility is for children to make animals with some moving parts as a technology project.

ASSEMBLY

- Teach the song.
- Let the group who have worked on the song demonstrate their actions to the others. In suitable situations, the other children can copy the actions or make up their own.
- **A thought**

  What a lot of different animals there are! And each one has its place, even ones that not everybody likes.

  Snails, for example. People who enjoy making their gardens look pretty don't like snails very much. Does anyone know why?... They eat plants. So a gardener puts out some young plants that he hopes will make lots of beautiful flowers in the summer. Then snails come and eat the plants so that they die. The gardener is not very happy!

  But snails also help gardeners. When they chew up leaves they turn them into compost. Compost is good for gardens and helps plants grow better.

Another strange thing is that snails are the favourite food of thrushes. Thrushes catch snails and break their shells on a stone. They eat their squashy insides. Yuk! Then the thrush goes and sits on the top of a tree or a chimney and sings a beautiful song. (Play bird-song tape, if you have one.) So plants get eaten by snails, snails get eaten by thrushes, and thrushes make lovely music in our gardens and streets. What a strange and wonderful world!

- The song can be sung again with the teacher or leader missing out the rhymes and the children supplying them.

BIBLE BACKGROUND

Look at the sea, so big and wide.
Its creatures large and small cannot be counted.
Psalm 104:25

BEARS WITH CLAWS

DRAW A CIRCLE WITH YOUR FINGER

Awareness of shapes, and the story of the healing of a blind man. Helps develop motor skills and works well with pupils with special needs.

RESOURCES

- Cards with shapes drawn on that will be used in the story: circle, square, wiggly cloud, tree (straight up, wiggly circle, straight down), eye outline (ellipse).

ASSEMBLY

◆ Sing the song, with appropriate actions.

A group or class can stand in a circle to sing with someone standing in the middle. On the last four lines she closes her eyes, points a finger, and turns in a circle on the spot, stopping at the end. The person pointed at then takes her place.

◆ Show the cards and help the children to draw these shapes in the air: circle, square, cloud, tree, eye.

◆ **A story: The man who thought people were trees**

Leader and children make shapes in the air to illustrate this story as it is told.

One day, Jesus and his friends were walking along the road by the Sea of Galilee. The *sun* shone in a bright blue sky and a few fluffy white *clouds* drifted on the warm breeze. There were lots of *trees* by the road. Some of them were *olive trees* that the people used to make oil for their lamps. Some were *fig trees* that had fruit that was good to eat.

Jesus and his friends arrived at a village called Bethsaida. In the village were lots of *square houses*. The houses had white walls and small *square windows*. Some of the ladies who lived in the village walked past carrying pots on their heads. They were going to the well to fetch water. The well had a *circle of stones* round it to stop children and animals from falling in.

When the people in the village saw that Jesus had come, some of them brought one of their friends to him. This man was blind. They said, 'Please, Jesus, touch our friend and make him better. Make him see again.'

Jesus took the man's hand and led him down the road. They went past the *square houses* and the *round well* until they were outside the village.

Then Jesus did something very strange. He put some spit on the man's *eyes* and laid his hands on him. Then he said to the man 'Open your *eyes*. Can you see now?'

The man opened his *eyes* and looked up. 'Yes!' he said. 'Yes! I can see things walking around. They must be people, but they look like *trees* to me.'

Jesus put his hands on the man's *eyes* again. 'Now look,' he said.

The man opened his *eyes*. They were completely healed and he could see everything clearly! He could see the *sun* in the sky. He could see the fluffy white *clouds*. He could see the *square houses* in the village and the well with the *round wall*. He could see the *olive trees* by the road. But now he knew they were *trees* and not people.

'Go home now,' said Jesus. And the man did. It was the happiest day in his life.

◆ As an extra touch, the cards could each have a smiley face on the back and be held by a line of children. At the end of the story, the children turn their cards round to show the happy faces.

BIBLE BACKGROUND

The story is found in Mark 8:22–26.

The man looked up and said, 'Yes, I see people, but they look like trees walking around.'

Mark 8:24

DRAW A CIRCLE

Not every child can always be chosen.
In this case, finish the song by changing the last line to:-
"....'till it reaches everybody now everyone's been found."
(making a big circle with your finger to cover everyone)

N.B.
Some children do enjoy standing up when they are chosen and performing the actions while the group sing.

ELIJAH
The story of Elijah, part 1

Dangers all around, and a story that shows that even grown-ups can do silly things when they should know better.

RESOURCES

- None essential. The story can be enhanced by using pieces of coloured cloth while telling it: green for the growing wheat, brown for the wooden idols, red for the sun, yellow for the dried-up plants, blue for the stream, black for the ravens. At the end, as a reminder of the story, the children can be shown the colours again and asked what they stood for.

ASSEMBLY

◆ Talk to the children about times they have played with toddlers. These could be younger brothers and sisters, or children of an aunt or neighbour.

Because they are big, responsible people, they know there are some things which are dangerous for toddlers or babies. With prompting, the children should be able to suggest some of these or others:

- marbles or other small objects that a toddler could choke on
- hot kettles and saucepans
- poisonous things in bottles that look like drinks
- tablets that look like sweets
- electric sockets
- running out into the road
- playing near water.

◆ Very young children don't know any better. We have to help look after them and tell a grown-up at once if we see them doing something that might harm them.

We do know better. What happens if we do something we know is dangerous, like running across the road? We get told off. We might be punished and sent to bed or not allowed to watch TV.

Grown-ups can do silly things when they should know better, too. There is a story in the Bible about a man who lived at a time when a lot of grown-ups were doing something silly when they should have known better. This man's name was Elijah.

- **The story of Elijah, part 1: The man who was fed by the birds.**

Elijah lived in Israel and worshipped God. He knew all the stories about how God had helped his people in the past. He knew the story of Noah and the animals in the ark. He knew the story about the baby Moses in the bulrushes. He knew the story about when God sent the plagues to Egypt and rescued the people from Pharaoh.

All the other people in Israel knew those stories, too. But instead of trusting God and worshipping him, lots of people had started worshipping an idol. An idol is just a carving made out of wood. People in Israel were worshipping an idol called Baal*. Baal was supposed to be the god of the weather. People thought that if they prayed to Baal he would send the rain to make the wheat grow. Elijah knew that that was silly. A piece of wood can't make it rain!

Elijah used to talk to God a lot. (That is what we call praying.) After lots of talking to God and listening quietly to what God was saying to him, Elijah decided to go and talk to the king of Israel. It was time to show people who was really the true God.

So Elijah went to talk to King Ahab. 'King Ahab,' he said, 'I serve the Lord, the God of Israel. You think Baal is the god of the weather, the one who sends the rain. But he isn't. He's just an idol made of wood. Now you are going to see who is the true God. For the next few years it is not going to rain at all unless I pray to God to make it rain.'

Elijah must have been very nervous when he had said that to King Ahab. But it happened just like he had said. That autumn, when the rains should have come, there was not even a shower. In the spring it was just the same, nothing but hot sunshine and scorching winds. Farmers planted their seeds, but the shoots shrivelled up and died. The people began to get worried. What were they going to eat if the crops didn't grow?

It wasn't safe for Elijah to be seen. King Ahab and his wife, Queen Jezebel, blamed him that there was no rain. Queen Jezebel was the one who had persuaded King Ahab to worship Baal. She had even killed lots of the prophets who worshipped God.

What should Elijah do? He prayed and listened to God. God told him to go away, to go where Ahab and Jezebel would not find him. So Elijah went to the

* Baal can be pronounced as *bail* or *barl.*

desert lands on the far side of the River Jordan. There was a rocky valley with a stream. Elijah camped in the valley, drinking water from the stream.

Living on the rocky ledges were some big, black birds called ravens. Ravens are like the crows we often see flying, only bigger. Every morning the ravens flew off to find food. In the evening they came back and dropped bits of bread and meat on the ground. Elijah picked up the food that the ravens dropped. It wasn't a feast, but it was enough to keep him from starving. Elijah knew God was looking after him.

Day after day it went on being hot and sunny. Elijah saw that the stream was getting smaller and smaller. Soon it would dry up altogether. Then what would he do?

Next time, we shall find out what happened when the stream dried up and Elijah had to go and find food and water somewhere else. After that, we shall hear about when God told Elijah to go and talk to King Ahab again, and how there was a big show-down.

- Teach the song.

BIBLE BACKGROUND

The story is found in 1 Kings 16:29–33 and 17:1–6.

Elijah was a man just like us. He prayed that it would not rain. And it did not rain on the land for three and a half years!

James 5:17

ELIJAH

To the tune of
Three Blind Mice
Traditional
C G C C G C
E- li- jah E- li- jah
G G7 C G G7 C
Nee- ded God Nee- ded God He
C G C C G C
knew that there would be no rain but God looked af- ter him just the same. His
C G C C G C
tum-my rum-bled the ra- vens came to E- li- jah.

DID YOU KNOW WHEN YOU'RE IN TROUBLE?
The story of Elijah, part 2

An experiment in sharing, and a story about how God helped a woman who shared.

RESOURCES

- An apple, a knife, and two plates.

ASSEMBLY

- Briefly remind the children of the first part of the story and sing the Elijah song.
- Elijah's tummy rumbled because he was hungry. We all know it is good to share, but when your tummy is rumbling and you are feeling very hungry it is much harder to share. Let's do an experiment with an apple and two people to help us.

  Core the apple and cut it into eight pieces. Give one volunteer who likes apples a plate with seven pieces of apple on it. Ask *Mark* what he had to eat yesterday, and what he had for breakfast today.

  Mark has had plenty to eat, and he is going to have his dinner today, and his tea when he gets home. Ask *Mark* if he would share his apple with some other people. He surely will not mind because it is just an extra little snack.

  Now get a second volunteer, one who likes apples and is feeling a bit hungry. Give *Annette* the plate with one piece of apple.

  This part of the experiment needs us to use our imagination. Let's imagine we hardly had anything to eat yesterday, just a little dried crust. We went to bed crying because we were so hungry our tummies hurt.

  Today we aren't going to have anything to eat at all. *Annette* has just one little piece of apple. It won't fill her hungry tum, but it is better than nothing. What would you do if you were *Annette*? Would you keep it and eat it yourself, or would you share it? Most of us would probably eat it ourselves, wouldn't we? What is *Annette* going to do?

We are going to hear about someone who was very hungry and had just a little to eat in our story.

◆ **The story of Elijah, part 2: The amazing jar of flour**

It hadn't rained for months and months. The little stream Elijah was camping by got smaller and smaller and then dried up altogether. Elijah knew he had to move.

He did not want to go back to Israel because he knew King Ahab and Queen Jezebel would be on the lookout for him. He talked to God, and God told him to go to another country, to a town with a funny name, Zarephath. There was someone there who would look after him.

Elijah set off on the long hot walk. When he finally arrived at the gates of Zarephath he was hungry and thirsty and exhausted. There was a woman near the gates picking up dry twigs to make a fire. This woman lived on her own with her little boy. Her husband had died, and there were just the two of them.

'Please,' said Elijah to the woman, 'I am so thirsty. Could you get me a cup of water?' As she turned to go, Elijah said, 'And bring me a piece of bread to eat, too.'

The woman looked at Elijah. 'The truth is,' she said, 'I haven't got any bread. All I have is a handful of flour at the bottom of the jar and a little oil in a jug. These sticks are to make a fire to cook our last piece of dry bread. When my son and I have eaten that, we shall have nothing left. We shall die of hunger.'

That was like *Annette* and her one piece of apple. Only this was real. This woman and her little boy couldn't go to the shops — they didn't have any money. There was no Giro coming in the post, because there weren't any in those days. They couldn't even borrow any food from the neighbours because everyone was keeping what little they had for themselves. It was what we call a famine, when the crops don't grow and there is nothing left to eat.

But Elijah knew the stories of how God had helped people in the past. He remembered how the ravens had brought scraps for him to eat. He said to the woman, 'Don't worry. Go home and cook the flour as you were going to. Only make me a roll of bread first. The God of Israel says, "Until it rains, that jar of flour will never become empty. The jug will always have oil in it."'

What would you have done? Would you have shared your last piece of bread with a stranger? Or would you have kept it for yourself and your little boy? What a hard question!

The Bible says that this woman did what Elijah told her to. And it says that what Elijah had told her came true. Every day there was still some flour left in the jar and some oil in the jug. Every day the woman and her son and

Elijah had enough to eat. She shared what little she had, and God rewarded her. They all lived through the famine.

Next time we shall hear what happened when God told Elijah to go to King Ahab again, and all about the show-down with the people who worshipped the idol, Baal.

- Elijah was in trouble when the stream ran dry and he needed food and drink. The woman was in trouble because she and her little boy looked like they were going to die of starvation. This is a song about asking God to help us when we are in trouble.

Teach the song.

BIBLE BACKGROUND

The story is found in 1 Kings 17:7–16.

The jar of flour and the jug of oil were never empty.
This happened just as the Lord, through Elijah, said it would.
1 Kings 17:16

DID YOU KNOW WHEN YOU'RE IN TROUBLE?

NOTHING'S IMPOSSIBLE WITH GOD
The story of Elijah, part 3

The story of one person's courage in standing alone and how that courage was rewarded.

RESOURCES

- None needed.

ASSEMBLY

- Briefly remind the children about Baal, the idol people thought was the god who sent the weather, and how Elijah had told King Ahab it would not rain until he said it would.
- **The story of Elijah, part 3: The big show-down**

That had been three years ago. For three years it hadn't rained in Israel. There was a famine in the whole country. King Ahab sent men out to all the places where there used to be springs and streams, hoping to find enough grass to keep his horses and donkeys alive.

Elijah was still living in the town with the funny name, Zarephath. The jar still had flour in it; the jug still had oil in it; the woman and her son still had food to eat every day.

Then one day, while Elijah was having his prayer time with God, God told him to go and meet King Ahab. He had a message for the king: it was going to rain soon.

Ahab wasn't pleased to see Elijah. 'You are the biggest trouble-maker in Israel,' he said to him.

'It's not me who is the trouble-maker,' replied Elijah. 'It is you and your family. You are the ones who have stopped listening to God. You are the ones who are worshipping the idol Baal. All this is your fault.

'Now I'm going to tell you what to do. Get all the people to come to the mountain called Mount Carmel. Make sure you bring the 450 prophets who worship Baal, and all the others who worship idols. I see that Queen Jezebel makes sure *they* have enough to eat, even though most of the people are starving.'

Ahab did what Elijah said. All the people gathered on the flat top of Mount Carmel, looking out over the scorched land below.

Elijah spoke to the people. 'It is time for you people to make up your minds,' he said in a big loud voice. 'Either the Lord who looked after us in the past is the true God, or this Baal is. They can't both be the true God. Now we are going to have a show-down. There are 450 prophets who worship Baal here, and there's just me on my own. Let's see which God answers our prayers.'

In those days people used to offer sacrifices to their gods. Elijah told the prophets of Baal to get wood for a fire and cut up a bull as a sacrifice. But they were not to set light to the fire. He was going to do the same with another bull. Then they would pray. The prophets would ask Baal, the weather god, to send a flash of lightning to set fire to the wood and burn their sacrifice. Elijah was going to pray to the Lord to send fire on his sacrifice.

Elijah told the prophets of Baal to go first, as there were lots of them. So the prophets of Baal prepared the wood and the bull. All morning they danced round the sacrifice and shouted, 'Baal, answer us! Send the fire!' But there was no sound. No one answered.

Elijah started to make fun of them. 'Perhaps Baal is thinking,' he said. 'Or perhaps he has gone away on a journey. Or maybe he's asleep. You'll have to shout louder to wake him up!'

So the prophets of Baal shouted louder. They danced more wildly. They did everything they could think of. But there was no lightning, no voice from the skies, nothing.

Then Elijah said to the people, 'Now it's my turn.' He took twelve big stones, one for each of the tribes of Israel, and made a kind of table from them, an altar to put the sacrifice on. The people watched as he dug a ditch all round it. Then he put the wood on the stones, and on the wood he put the meat from the bull.

'Now,' said Elijah, 'I want four of you to go down the hill to the spring with your water pots. Fill them up and come and pour the water on the meat and the wood.' He got them to do that three times, until the wood was all soaking and the water filled the ditch.

Then Elijah started talking to God. 'I know you are the God of our father Abraham,' he said. 'You are the God who always looked after Israel, our ancestor who gave his name to our people. I ask you now to prove that you are the true God. Show these people that it is you who control the weather, and everything else.'

As Elijah was praying, there was a flash from the sky. The wood on the stones caught fire. It burned so fiercely that all the meat was burned up and the water in the ditch turned to steam. When all the people saw this, they realised how foolish they had been. For years they had been wasting their time worshipping an idol made of wood. They fell on the ground. 'The Lord is the true God!' they cried out. 'The Lord is the true God!'

A few hours later, black clouds began to fill the sky. The wind started to blow, and at last it began to pour with rain. It was the first rain for three and a half years. The people went back to their homes through the rain. They were happy and sad all at the same time. They were happy it was raining, because now the grass would grow and they could plant new crops. But they were sad because they had listened to the prophets of Baal, and that was why the famine had come in the first place.

King Ahab had to hurry home in his chariot before it got bogged down in the mud. When he told Queen Jezebel what had happened, she was furious. She knew the people would not listen to her any more. She sent a message to Elijah. 'I'm going to kill you for what you have done,' she said. 'By this time tomorrow you are going to be dead!'

Next time we shall find out what happened to Elijah. Did Queen Jezebel get him, or did he escape? You'll have to wait to find out.

◆ Teach the song.

BIBLE BACKGROUND

The story is found in 1 Kings 18 and 19:1–2.

How long will you try to serve both Baal and the Lord? If the Lord is the true God, follow him. But if Baal is the true God, follow him!

Elijah in 1 Kings 18:21

NOTHING'S IMPOSSIBLE WITH GOD

Other suggestions relative to our lives today:

He can find new friends, to love you ...
When we're afraid, He'll lead us to safety ...

GOD DOESN'T ONLY SPEAK IN THE THUNDER

The story of Elijah, part 4

The importance of stillness and careful listening.

RESOURCES

- Rig up a cloth as a screen. Sounds are going to be made behind this screen and children have to guess what the sounds are. Other items as in the list of suggestions below. The sounds you can use will depend to some extent on the size of the group.

ASSEMBLY

◆ Explain that you (or, better, an assistant) are going to make some sounds behind the screen. The children have to guess what is happening to make each of the sounds. They will have to be absolutely still and quiet to hear the sounds.

Suggestions:

- sharpening a pencil
- pouring a glass of water
- striking a match
- stirring a drink with a spoon
- flicking the pages of a book
- brushing teeth
- opening and eating a packet of crisps
- stapling some sheets of paper together.

Congratulate the children on their attentiveness and guesses. Now they will have to listen quietly to the last part of the story of Elijah. There is a lot of noise in this story, but the important bit is something very quiet. Find out what it is.

◆ **The story of Elijah, part 4: Elijah learns an important lesson**

After the show-down on Mount Carmel, Queen Jezebel was so angry that she sent a message to tell Elijah that he had only one day to live. Elijah was scared. He knew the queen meant what she said. He ran away to save his life.

He set off on a long journey, all the way to another mountain, a very special mountain for the Israelites. It was Mount Sinai. The Israelites called it 'The Mountain of God'.

Elijah knew the story of what happened on Mount Sinai. When Moses was leading the children of Israel out of slavery in Egypt, they stopped at the bottom of Mount Sinai. Moses went to talk to God on the mountain. It was there that God gave Moses the Ten Commandments. Elijah needed to talk to God now. It took him six weeks of walking to get there.

Elijah found a cave to shelter in on the mountain. Although he had won the show-down on Mount Carmel, when God sent fire on the sacrifice, he was feeling very unhappy. 'Lord God,' he prayed, 'I have always tried to serve you the best I could. But everyone else deserted you. Jezebel killed all the prophets who believed in you. I am the only one left. And now Jezebel is trying to kill me, too.'

Elijah stopped. He had never felt so miserable. He felt like giving up. He wanted God to talk to him and tell him what to do.

He felt God telling him to go and stand on the mountain. A strong wind began to blow. It grew stronger and stronger until it howled round the mountain and even sent rocks crashing down. Elijah was frightened. He clung on and listened. Was God trying to tell him something in the wind? No, nothing. God wasn't in the wind.

Then the earth started to shake. It was an earthquake! More rocks came crashing down. Was God trying to tell him something in the earthquake? No, nothing. God wasn't in the earthquake.

Then the dry trees and bushes on the mountain caught fire. There was a roar of flames. Elijah hid in the cave. Was God trying to tell him something in the fire? No, nothing. God wasn't in the fire.

Then it all went very still and very quiet. There was nothing but a gentle whisper. This time, Elijah knew God was saying something to him. He went to the entrance to the cave and listened very carefully.

'You think you are the only one left,' God said to Elijah. 'But you aren't. There are 7,000 people living in Israel who still believe in me. There are 7,000 people who never worshipped the idol Baal.'

Then Elijah realised that God was teaching him an important lesson. Sometimes God did big things that everyone could see, like stopping the rain for three years, or sending fire on the sacrifice. But most of the time he didn't do big things like that. Most of the time he just worked quietly. He had been quietly speaking to 7,000 people in Israel all the time, people who still believed in him. Elijah wasn't alone, after all.

'Now I've got another job for you to do,' God said to Elijah. 'I have chosen a man to be the new king of Israel instead of Ahab. And I have chosen a man called Elisha to be my prophet when you are gone. Go and find them and tell them I have chosen them.'

So Elijah did what God said. He had learned an important lesson. There will always be people who do wrong things, like King Ahab and Queen Jezebel and the prophets of Baal. There will always be stupid people who listen to them and do what they say. But there will always be people who know better — good people, people who listen to the quiet voice of God talking to them.

Clever people know it is important to be quiet sometimes, to learn to listen. We never know when God might have an important lesson to teach us, just like he taught Elijah.

◆ Use the song to underline the message.

BIBLE BACKGROUND

The story is found in 1 Kings 19:1–18.

In quietness and trust is your strength. Isaiah 30:15

◆ **More...**

There could be a fifth, recap, assembly, using all the songs and perhaps a quiz on the story.

GOD DOESN'T ONLY SPEAK IN THE THUNDER

FLAP YOUR WINGS

We stay safe by listening to our parents and doing what they tell us; the parallel of God's care for us.

RESOURCES

- A large cloak, or improvise one from a piece of heavy material; a 'nest' of hay or cloth with five hen's eggs in it.

ASSEMBLY

- Show the children the 'nest' with the eggs inside. Talk about how mother hens sit on the eggs to keep them warm until they hatch. When the chicks do hatch the mother hen looks after them very carefully. If there is danger, the little chicks run and hide under her wings.

  Put on the cloak and choose one or two children to sit either side of you under the cloak, like chicks under the mother's wings.

- **A story: Brave Little Chick**

  Mother Hen wiggled her bottom and settled down carefully on the five eggs in the hay. For ten days she had been keeping them warm under her soft feathers so that the baby chicks inside could grow and grow. Now they were almost ready to hatch. 'Cheep, cheep! Cheep, cheep!' went the little chicks inside the eggs as they got ready to come into the big world.

  Curled up inside the shells, the chicks were beginning to feel uncomfortable. They wanted to stretch their new wings and try their legs, but there just wasn't enough room. They didn't need anyone to tell them what to do, though. 'Peck, peck!' they went on the hard shell with their tough little beaks. 'Peck, peck!'

  'Tap, tap!' was the sound Mother Hen heard. 'Tap, tap! Cheep, cheep!' Not long now, she thought.

  A little crack appeared on one shell, then on another. 'Tap, tap! Peck, peck!' More cracks appeared, then little bits of shell started to fall off. The baby chicks certainly knew what to do now: tap harder, wiggle their wings and their legs; push off the bits of shell.

At last one of the chicks had done it. He sat exhausted on the bits of broken shell, just a skinny little chick with soggy feathers. He looked a mess, but he didn't care. He'd done it! He had made it out into the big wide world. He was a Brave Little Chick.

Father Rooster flew up and stood on top of a tree stump. He ruffled his feathers, showed off his beautiful coloured tail, stretched his neck, and let out the biggest crow he could. 'Cock-a-doodle-doo!' he crowed proudly. 'Cock-a-doodle-doo! I'm a new father. I've got five new baby chicks. Cock-a-doodle-dooooo!'

The next day Mother Hen led her five babies out into the chicken run. They weren't wet and bedraggled any longer, but fluffy and yellow with strong little orange legs and beady black eyes. 'Peck, peck!' went Mother Hen on some scraps of ground-up corn, showing her babies what to do. They all ran to start pecking in the same place, learning how to feed themselves.

Father Rooster stood on his tree stump with his chest puffed out and the red comb on his head glowing in the morning sun. He watched Mother Hen showing her chicks where to find food and how to drink water from a special chick-sized trough. But he was watching something else, too. He was watching the small hole in a dark corner of the chicken run where Mister Rat lived.

Mister Rat was a thief. When nobody was looking he would creep out and steal the corn, greedily gobbling it down until his cheeks swelled up. He would steal the precious eggs, too, if he got a chance. But Father Rooster knew he could do worse than that. He knew Mister Rat would love nothing more than to catch one of the baby chicks and drag it down into his dark hole, never to be seen again.

Suddenly, there it was: a shiny black nose sniffing the morning air, stiff white whiskers twitching hungrily. Mister Rat wanted his breakfast, too. Father Rooster let out an angry squawk and flew down from his perch. He flapped his strong wings to frighten the thief away. Mother Hen clucked a warning to her babies and quickly gathered them underneath her wings. It was safe there, a warm, dark place hidden away among her cosy brown feathers.

'Listen,' clucked Mother Hen to her babies when the danger was past. 'The world is full of good things to enjoy, but full of dangers, too. There are rats who hide, waiting to pounce. There are foxes who come by night. There are hawks who swoop from high up in the sky. You can never be too careful. Don't go far away. And whenever you hear me clucking "Danger! Danger!", come running as quick as ever you can and hide under my wings. Then you will be safe.'

The five chicks listened wide-eyed to their mother. Little heads peeped out from among her feathers and disappeared again. Was it safe to come out?

Had Mister Rat gone? Was there anything in the sky except the friendly warm sun? Little by little they got brave enough to come out and start pecking the food again.

Brave Little Chick was more adventurous than all the others. He looked up at Father Rooster on his perch. 'One day I'm going to be like that,' he thought. 'I'm going to have shiny green and black feathers, and a big curved tail, and a fine red comb on my head. I'm going to sit on a tree stump and crow so loudly that Mister Rat will never dare come out of his hole.'

Thinking like that made him feel even more brave. He started exploring on his own, going further and further away from Mother Hen and his four brothers and sisters. Mother Hen kept clucking to him not to go too far, but Brave Little Chick didn't want to listen. There were good things to eat, and new places to find, and interesting things to see.

Suddenly there was a loud squawk and a flutter and an anxious clucking: 'Danger! Danger! Come quick! Danger!' Four little chicks scrambled to safety under Mother Hen's warm wings. Four? But there should have been... five. Where was chick number five? Where was Brave Little Chick? Father Rooster's head jerked round looking for him. By the feeding trough? No. By the scratchy place in the sun? No. By the old tree stump? No. By the hole in the dark corner? Oh!... Yes!

And right in front of him was Mister Rat, his white whiskers twitching, his shiny black nose sniffing, his long sharp teeth all ready to grab the fluffy yellow chick. It was Brave Little Chick to be sure, only he wasn't brave any longer. He was so frightened his orange legs were shaking like jelly. He could not move a single step. Mister Rat's mouth opened wide, and then... Flap! [Clap hands.]

There was a sudden flurry of wings as Father Rooster dived from his perch and landed right on Mister Rat's nose. Brave Little Chick got bowled over and over like a scrap of yellow paper in the wind. As soon as he could find his feet he ran as fast as he could to hide under Mother Hen's safe wings. It took him a long time to stop trembling. And it took a long time for the fluffy feathers he had lost to float down to the ground like yellow snowflakes.

Perhaps we shouldn't call him Brave Little Chick at all. Perhaps we should call him Foolish Little Chick. He very nearly didn't grow up to have shiny black and green feathers like Father Rooster, or a proud curved tail, or a fine red comb on his head. But Brave Little Chick never went near the hole in the dark corner again. From then on, he only did his exploring close by where he could run for safety under Mother Hen's warm wings.

All through the summer he grew and grew. And when the autumn leaves had blown through the pen, and when the real snow of winter had come and gone,

one fine day Brave Little Chick stepped out into the spring sunshine. Only he wasn't a little chick any longer. Now he was Brave Young Rooster, all ready to start a family of his own. He flew up on the tree stump and gave a mighty proud crow. 'Cock-a-doodle-doo! Watch out, Mister Rat, you'd better not show your nose round here! Cock-a-doodle-doo!'

◆ That was a scary story. We had better make sure that *we* are not Foolish Little Chicks, but Clever Little Children who listen to their parents and keep out of danger.

Here is a song to make us smile. It is a song about Jesus' love for us. One day Jesus spoke to some people who thought they were very brave, but were really very foolish. He said he longed to look after them, just like 'a hen gathers her chicks under her wings'. He wanted to help them, but they would not listen to him. We are not like that, are we?

Sing the song, 'Flap your wings'.

BIBLE BACKGROUND

'Jerusalem, Jerusalem!... I wanted to help your people.
I wanted to gather them together as a hen gathers her chicks under her wings.
But you did not let me.'

Jesus in Luke 13:34

FLAP YOUR WINGS

Begin slowly. Repeat doing the actions getting faster.

FOLLOW 'J' FOR JESUS

An introduction to some of the most famous teaching in the world, including some essential social skills.

RESOURCES

- Write the letters J (upper case), l, f, k, d and p (lower case) on pieces of paper to hold up.

ASSEMBLY

- Show the J for Jesus and teach the song.
- **5 things Jesus told his followers to do**

  Jesus lived with the family of his friend Peter in a town called Capernaum by the beautiful Sea of Galilee.

  One of the places Jesus loved to go to was a hill near the town. Jesus would climb the steep hill and sit in the long grass on the top. Spread out before him was the blue-grey water and the hills of Galilee disappearing in the haze. In the early spring the grass was green and full of colourful wild flowers. By summer it was brown and dry. But it was still a good place to go and be quiet. Jesus liked to go there early in the morning to pray, to talk to his Father in heaven.

  It wasn't always quiet, though. People from Capernaum and villages nearby knew it was one of Jesus' favourite places and they would come there to find him. Other people came as well, some of them from many miles away.

  One day a great crowd of people gathered there, sitting on the steep hillside where they could see Jesus and hear his stories. He decided this was a good time to teach them about being his followers. What he taught them has become very famous. People call it, **The Sermon on the Mount**. Here are some of the things Jesus told his followers to do.

  (Hold up the 'l'.) **l** is for **love everyone**. Jesus told his followers to love other people, even those who aren't nice to them.[1] Get the children to repeat: 'l is for love everyone'.

  (Hold up the 'f'.) **f** is for **forgive one another**. Jesus told his followers to forgive other people when they have been nasty to them.[2]

(Hold up the 'k'.) **k** is for **keep God's commands**. A command is when someone tells someone else what to do, like an officer in the army giving a command to a soldier. Jesus told his followers to do all the things God tells them to do.[3]

(Hold up the 'd'.) **d** is for **don't call people names**. Jesus told his followers not to say bad things about people or call them names.[4]

(Hold up the 'p'.) **p** is for **pray for other people**. Jesus told his followers to pray for other people, especially those who hurt them.[5]

Go through the five letters again until the children can remember what each one stands for.

BIBLE BACKGROUND

1. **But I say to you, love your enemies.** Matthew 5:44

2. **Forgive us our sins, just as we have forgiven those who sinned against us.** Matthew 6:12

3. **Whoever obeys the commands... will be great in the kingdom of heaven.** Matthew 5:19

4. **If you say bad things to a brother or sister, you will be judged by the council.** Matthew 5:22

5. **Pray for those who hurt you.** Matthew 5:44

- **More...**
- For a further assembly, recap on the five things Jesus told his followers to do in the Sermon on the Mount.
- Jesus knew that these were very hard things to do and that people needed help to do them. He taught them a special prayer which asks God to help them do the hard things.

Christians call this prayer, The Lord's Prayer. Teach it to the children. It can be found in Matthew 6:9–13.

A suitable song to sing: 'We Make People Happy When We Pray'.

FOLLOW JESUS

GIMME FIVE

Greetings from around the world and what they mean.

RESOURCES

- A Hawaiian *lei*, the traditional garland of flowers, could be made.

ASSEMBLY

- What do we say to each other when we start assembly? Good morning (or whatever). What do we say when we meet our friends in the morning? Hello. All over the world people have different ways of greeting each other, of saying hello.

  Children could be asked which they know. They might be brought out to the front to teach the others how to say 'hello' in a language they know.

  Examples: American — hi or howdy; Australian — g'day; French — bonjour; German — guten tag; Spanish — hola; Hebrew — shalom; Arabic — salaam.

  As well as words, there are actions. Examples to show or try: shake hands; slap hands; kiss on the cheeks; hug; bow (Japanese); rub noses (Eskimo).

  All these words and actions really mean the same thing. They are all ways of saying: 'I'm your friend. I want to be nice to you and I hope you are going to be nice to me.'

  Sometimes there are ways of greeting someone special. On the island of Hawaii people make garlands of flowers. This is called a *lei.* It is placed around the neck of a visitor to make them feel really welcome and special. (A *lei* could be used in school to make someone feel special.)

  What do people do if they meet the Queen? Bow or curtsey. Some Christians bow in church. They bow before the altar at the front of the church because they want to honour Jesus as the greatest king of all.

  Another thing some Christians do in church is to greet each other with the words, 'Peace be with you' and shake hands or hug each other.

- Teach the song. It can also be said as a rap.

- Different greetings might be used in succeeding assemblies. Eg 'What country shall we be today? Australian? G'day, everybody.'

BIBLE BACKGROUND

Before you go into a house, say, 'Peace be with this house.'

Jesus in Luke 10:5

GIMME FIVE

Alternative rap style:

Gimme five, gimme five, gimme fi-fi-five,
'Cause Jesus is alive.
Give a shake, give a shake, give a shake, shake, shake,
'Cause He died for my sake.
Give a bow, give a bow, give a bow, bow, bow,
If you want to show Him how
We worship Jesus the King.

GOD GAVE NOAH A JOB TO DO

A lovely song to use when a child achieves something, no matter how small; good for building self-esteem.

RESOURCES

- None needed.

ASSEMBLY

- If children know the story of Noah, briefly recap on it. (Otherwise tell the story and use the song at the end. Follow up with these ideas subsequently.)
- Teach the song.
- God gave Noah a very important job to do because he was a good man and did what God told him to do. But it is not just famous people like Noah. God gives us all jobs to do, every day. Here are some of the jobs God gives us to do:
  - come to school and learn new things
  - practise what we know and get better
  - do what our parents tell us to
  - be helpful at school and at home
  - be friendly to each other
  - look after the world God has given us.

  Plus whatever specific tasks are currently appropriate, eg:
  - write our names
  - spell words without looking
  - make a clever model.
- Ask staff to name a child who has recently done one of these 'jobs'. Bring child to the front and sing the song using the child's name in place of Noah. Eg 'God gave Clare a job to do... and she did what she was told.' Repeat as many times as desirable.

Note. This song can also be used with the story of Jonah. It is a nice song to sing when a teacher leaves, or as a 'thank you' to a visitor.

BIBLE BACKGROUND

Children, obey your parents the way the Lord wants.
This is the right thing to do.

The Apostle Paul in Ephesians 6:1

GOD GAVE NOAH A JOB TO DO

A good song to use for congratulating someone for doing a good job.

Also useful when teaching other stories from the Bible.

A

GOD MADE OUR BODIES BEAUTIFUL

Teaching on a part of our bodies linked to a warning on taking practical jokes too far. Can be used at Hallowe'en.

RESOURCES

- A balloon and pin. A picture of a heart (organ) might be used.

ASSEMBLY

- What happens if you get a fright, say someone jumps out from behind a door and goes 'Boo!', or if there is a sudden loud bang? It makes you jump. Your heart starts beating loud and fast, going 'boom, boom, boom'.

  Who can show us where your heart is? Your heart is a muscle, like the ones in your arms. It is a very special muscle. It is about the size of your fist. Who knows what it does? It pumps. It keeps squeezing and letting go. When it squeezes, it pumps blood all round your body. Blood is very important. Our bodies can't work without it.

  When we have a fright, our bodies say, 'Quick! We might need to run away from danger. We need extra blood. Pump harder, heart, and send the blood round extra fast.' So the heart pumps harder, and we feel it going 'boom, boom, boom'.

  Some people enjoy having a bit of a fright. It even makes them laugh. Babies often like playing the game where someone hides their face and then appears and says, 'Boo!' If you have played that game with a baby you know that if you shout too loud it makes them cry. You have to get it just right.

  Here is a balloon. Some people enjoy popping balloons. Others don't like it at all. Hands up who likes it? Hands up who doesn't like it?

  Depending on the group, talking about it may be enough. Some people's hearts will be beating faster just thinking about it. If appropriate, ask those who don't mind bangs to close their eyes and keep them closed while you walk quietly behind someone. Those who don't like bangs can keep their eyes open and watch. Pop the balloon. Ask the children to feel their hearts. Whose heart is beating louder and faster?

Your heart beats faster because your body is getting ready to run away from danger. The danger might be a car coming when you are in the middle of the road. It might be something falling down that could hit you. You need to run quickly to safety.

If it is a bad fright you might start shivering and shaking. Your face might go white. You might start crying. Your hair might even stand on end. All those things are good if there is real danger. Your body is looking after itself. But it is not nice to make people feel like that for a joke.

So let us say 'thank you' for our bodies and for our hearts that go 'boom, boom, boom' when we get a fright. They are very clever.

- If appropriate, talk about Hallowe'en or another situation where people may go too far.
- Teach the song. Use whichever verses are appropriate. The chorus can be repeated, getting quieter and quieter each time — good for settling a group down.

BIBLE BACKGROUND

A person shouldn't trick his neighbour and then say, 'I was just joking!' That is like a madman shooting deadly, burning arrows.

Proverbs 26:18–19

GOD MADE OUR BODIES BEAUTIFUL

2. D'ya think that knocking at the doors of strangers,
   Is a very safe thing to do?
   When you make someone jump, does their heart go bump?
   So is that a good thing to do?

3. Do you really enjoy feeling frightened?
   Or making people feel that way?
   Would you rather be cheerful, or horribly fearful
   At the end of every day?

Use pause on first note to get everyone's attention.

A C (P)

HAVE YOU EVER TRIED REACHING FOR THE SKY?

Trying new things — and doing our very best — is a vital part of life.

RESOURCES

- Pieces of work, or art, or CDT children have done.

CLASS PREPARATION (Optional)

- Talk about some of the new things people have done, as below, and get ready to talk about them in assembly, to show pieces of work, etc.

ASSEMBLY

- Sing some of the verses of the song.
- If a class has prepared the assembly, they can talk about new things they have done or achieved.

  Otherwise ask children for examples of new things they have tried, such as:

  - something new to eat or drink
  - a new place they have been to
  - a new friend
  - a new programme on TV
  - a new song
  - something new they have learned in school or elsewhere.

  Staff might add their own examples, showing that even as adults we never stop learning or discovering new things.

  That is also true of God. Even though God was there before the world began, it says in the Bible that he does new things, too.

- Talk about someone in the news, someone who has achieved something noteworthy, or about the singer of a popular song that the children know. That person was a five-year-old at school once. There was a first time he or she kicked a ball, or sang a song (or whatever skill has been demonstrated in their achievement). When we try something new, we don't know where it will lead to. 'Reaching for the sky' is also a way of saying, 'doing the very best I can'. That means everybody should try 'reaching for the sky'.

- Sing the song again. New verses could be added. A final verse such as 'keeping very still' is a way of finishing quietly.

BIBLE BACKGROUND

Look at the new thing I am going to do.
It is already happening. Don't you see it?
The Lord in Isaiah 43:19

HAVE YOU EVER TRIED?

This song is very adaptable.

Some suggestions for other verses:-

putting on a hat
standing on your toes
shaking someone's hand
giving a smile
laughing out loud
whistling a tune
blowing a kiss
counting up to five
writing your name ***(in the air)***
pulling a cracker ***(for Christmas)***

HELP ME GET UP IN THE MORNING

We all need help from others — and we can help them, too. The song is a simple way of introducing children to prayer.

RESOURCES

- Various common items — see the suggestions below.

ASSEMBLY

◆ Choose children to come to the front and do a number of simple tasks. For each, choose one child to begin with, then observe that he or she will need help. Choose another child to help. Suggestions:

- Hold up a long picture, banner, or piece of material. It needs one at each end.
- Move a bench. It is too heavy and awkward for one person alone.
- Put on a dress with buttons down the back. (If you don't have a suitable dress, use a shirt or blouse back to front and imagine it is a dress.) The wearer needs help with the buttons.
- Tie a knot in a piece of string round a parcel. (It is probably best to do this yourself.) A helper is needed to put their finger on the knot to keep it tight.
- Scratch an itch in the middle of the back.
- Plait hair.
- Hold a skipping rope for someone else to skip with. It needs one at each end.
- Stand with a book balanced on the head. Then bend down and pick up a second book from the floor and put it on the first without dropping the first. Very difficult unless a friend picks it up and puts it on for you.

◆ Lots and lots of things are too hard or even impossible for us to do on our own. We all need people to help us lots of times every day. And we can help other people lots of times every day, too.

Sometimes things are not only too hard for us, they are too hard for anyone to help us with either. Then we have a real problem.

There was once a man who had a problem like that. In fact, he had *two* problems like that. The first problem was because his son was ill and no one could make him better. The second problem was inside his own head. Problems inside your head can be the hardest problems of all. This is the story.

- **A story: The man who needed help**

This man lived a long time ago. He lived at the same time as Jesus, and three of Jesus' friends tell what happened to him in the stories we call the Gospels.

Even though his son was no longer a child, the boy could not talk. Not only that, but sometimes he had fits and fell on the ground, foaming at the mouth and grinding his teeth. Sometimes when he had a fit, he fell into the fire or into some water. The man had to watch his son all day long to make sure he didn't have a serious accident. He was worn out from looking after him. No one was able to help him make his son better. What could he do?

One day he saw a crowd of people who were waiting for Jesus. When Jesus arrived, the man went to ask Jesus to help him. 'If you can do anything for my son, please have pity on us and help us,' he said to Jesus.

Jesus said to the boy's father, 'You said, "*If* you can!" It's not a matter of "if". Anything is possible for the person who believes.'

Then the man realised he had another problem. This was the problem inside his head. He sort of believed Jesus could do something to help his son, but he wasn't *really, really sure* Jesus could make him better.

'I do believe!' the man cried out to Jesus. 'Please help me to believe more!'

Jesus did help him. He knew what was wrong with the man's son. Straightaway he made the boy better, and helped him to stand up. That must have been the happiest day in the father's life.

- So Jesus helped that man with two problems that no one else could help him with. No one could make his son better, but Jesus did. He also had the problem inside his head. He half believed Jesus could do something, but he wasn't really sure. He asked Jesus to help him believe more.

We often have problems inside our heads, too. We might be frightened of something, like being frightened of the dark. Like the father in the story, we can ask Jesus to help us.

Or we might do something stupid and we know we should say sorry, but somehow the words won't come out.

Or we might feel lonely and want a friend.

Here is a song that is a prayer. It asks Jesus to help us. You can use this song any time you want to and make up your own words.

- Teach the song.

BIBLE BACKGROUND

The story is found in Mark 9:14–29.

Immediately the father cried out, 'I do believe! Help me to believe more!'
Mark 9:24

HELP ME GET UP IN THE MORNING

2. **Help me be kind to others.**
3. **Help me make friends at school.**
4. **Help me to say 'thank you'.**
5. **Help me to say 'sorry'.**
6. **Help me feel safe at night.**

P

HOW DO WE GET FROM EARTH TO HEAVEN?

Some thoughts on a tricky question: Where is heaven and how do we get there?

RESOURCES

- Children's artwork.

CLASS PREPARATION

- Talk about transport; find, draw or paint pictures of different forms of transport; make models.

ASSEMBLY

- Ask questions like, 'Who can draw a car / paint a boat / make a model of a plane?' etc. Show examples produced by children.

  Now, who can make a *real* car? No one here. Who can make a *real* ship to sail in over the sea, or a *real* plane to fly in? No one here. We can paint pictures and make models, but we need grown-ups to make real ones, lots of grown-ups in special factories.

  If there are children whose parents work in any of these industries, or build boats, etc. as a hobby, children could talk about these.

  But there is something even grown-ups can't make. They can't make a rocket to go to heaven. They can make rockets to go to the moon or to Mars, but they can't make a rocket to go to heaven.

  Do you know what Jesus said to grown-ups? He said to them, 'If you want to get to heaven, you have to be like children!' Grown-ups can make cars and trains and planes to visit grandma or go to Disneyland, but they have to learn from children about how to get to heaven.

  Jesus said that heaven is so close it's right where you are. You don't need a rocket. You don't have to travel anywhere to find it. But you can't see it, not with your eyes. You can only 'see' it with your heart. And grown-ups often find it hard to believe in things they can't see.

◆ **A true story**

A little girl was very sick and although the doctors had done everything they could, they could not make her better. Her mummy and daddy were with her as she was dying. The last thing she said to them was, 'An angel is coming to get me. You can't see the angel, can you? But I can see him.'

The girl died, and her mummy and daddy were very sad. But they knew she had gone to heaven, and that one day they would see her again. They couldn't see the angel, but she had seen it. That helped them a lot.

◆ **A prayer**

Father God, help us to see with our hearts and to find heaven. And perhaps we can teach grown-ups to see it, too.

BIBLE BACKGROUND

The kingdom of God is near.

Jesus in Mark 1:15

I tell you the truth, you must accept God's kingdom like a little child, or you will never enter it!

Jesus in Luke 18:17

On ne voit bien qu'avec le coeur. L'essentiel est invisible aux yeux. Antoine de St Exupery, *Le Petit Prince.*

HOW DO WE GET FROM EARTH TO HEAVEN?

This is a good song to use to teach basic music knowledge in scales.

M (P)

I AM A ROBOT

A fun way to learn about the way God made us.

RESOURCES

- A selection of 'feelings' pictures from pages 180–190.
- Craft materials, if some children are to prepare robot costumes.
- Percussion instruments.

CLASS PREPARATION (Optional)

- Some children could make robot costumes from boxes, etc., and practise moving like robots.

ASSEMBLY

- Teach the song.
- The robot says, 'I've got no feelings. Kids are different.' Real people have feelings. Let's think about some of the feelings we have.

  Show selection of 'feelings' faces. Ask the children to identify and name the feelings. Get them to copy the faces and to imagine the feelings inside them.
- The robot says, 'Kids are different, you see, because you're made by God to be just like Jesus, not like me.' God made us to have feelings, just like Jesus did.

  Sometimes Jesus was happy (show happy face), like the time he went to a wedding. There was a party that lasted several days. Jesus joined in the celebrations and dancing. He enjoyed himself with the other guests at the wedding.

  Sometimes he was upset (show tearful face), like the time when his friend Lazarus died. Jesus heard the news that Lazarus was sick. He went to the village where Lazarus lived with his two sisters. When he got there, Lazarus was dead. Jesus cried, just like we do when something very sad happens. Then he made Lazarus come alive again.

  Sometimes he was angry (show angry face), like the time he found traders cheating people at the temple in Jerusalem. The traders had market stalls to sell things people needed when they came to the temple to worship God. But they cheated people by charging prices that were much too high. Jesus got angry and knocked their stalls over. He said they were turning God's house into a robbers' den.

We get feelings like that, too, because we are not robots. God made us to be like Jesus. Sometimes something makes us happy. Sometimes something makes us upset or frightened and we cry. Sometimes something makes us angry. It is good to have feelings like these, much better than being a robot.

- Sing the song again. It works well accompanied by a percussion group. A slide-whistle is good for the failing battery. Children with costumes can do robot movements.

This is a good song for involving boys in musical movement.

BIBLE BACKGROUND

God created human beings in his image.
Genesis 1:27

I AM A ROBOT

This is a great song to use with percussion instruments.

I CAN MAKE MYSELF BIG

A story that helps children identify feelings and teaches about different sorts of behaviour — rude and caring.

RESOURCES

- Copies of the 'feelings' faces from pages 180–190 showing Jesus frowning and caring; Simon frowning and angry; Woman tearful and happy.

ASSEMBLY

◆ **A story: The man who was rude**

Jesus was visiting a village one day when he was invited by an important person to have tea. The person's name was Simon, and he lived in a big house with white walls and a shady yard. The food was served outside in the courtyard because that was a good place to be on a hot day.

Now you would think that was very nice, but actually it wasn't as good as it sounds. You see, Simon was really a rather rude person. I think he looked like this. (Show Simon frowning face.) He wanted to hear what Jesus had to say, but he didn't do any of the polite things people usually did in that country to make guests feel welcome.

People usually gave guests water to wash their feet after walking in sandals down hot, dirty roads. Simon didn't give Jesus any water. People usually gave their guests a welcoming hug. Simon didn't give Jesus a hug. People usually gave their guests some nice-smelling oil to put on their hair to make them look smart. Simon didn't give Jesus anything to make his hair look nice. As I said, he was really rather rude.

Jesus and Simon and a few of Simon's friends sat around a square table. There were dates and figs and nuts and flat golden loaves of bread for them to eat. They didn't sit on chairs like ours, but stretched out on couches with their feet up, leaning on one elbow. Other people came into the courtyard to see what was going on, and because they were curious about Jesus.

One of these people was a woman who was crying. (Show Woman tearful face.) She had come specially to see Jesus, so she went and stood behind him. She was crying so much that big tears splashed down on Jesus' feet. When she saw that Jesus' feet were getting wet with her tears, she took the comb out of her long hair and let it down and dried his feet with it. She even kissed them. Then she took out some expensive perfume she had brought with her and rubbed that on his feet.

What do you think Simon's face was like when he saw this? Well, if he was frowning before, it was even worse now! He didn't like this woman at all. People said she did bad things. He would never, ever invite her to his house, and he was cross that she had come into his courtyard. Now he looked like this. (Show Simon angry face.)

But Jesus wasn't frowning, or angry. He looked like this. (Show Jesus caring face.) How do you think he was feeling? Kind and caring. He knew this woman was really sorry for the bad things she had done. He knew that she wanted to change and be different. He knew that people like Simon were often nasty to her. Jesus also knew that this woman loved him because he wasn't rude and nasty like Simon, but he really cared for people like her.

So Jesus told Simon off. I think it was Jesus' turn to look like this now. (Show Jesus frowning face.) 'You didn't give me any water to wash my feet,' he said to Simon, 'but this woman has washed them with her own tears. You didn't give me a hug to welcome me, but she has even kissed my feet. You didn't give me any oil for my hair, but she has put expensive perfume on my feet.'

'Now I'm going to tell you something else, Simon,' said Jesus. 'You think this woman has done lots of bad things. But all the bad things she has done have been forgiven. It's like she never did anything bad in her whole life. I know it's true because of her tears and the way she showed she loved me.'

Then Jesus turned to the woman behind him and smiled, a warm, kind smile. 'You don't need to worry about the bad things you have done any more,' he said. 'Your sins are forgiven. Go in peace.'

How do you think the woman looked now? Do you think she looked like this? (Show Woman happy face.)

And what about Simon? Do you think he felt ashamed because he had been so rude? Or do you think he felt cross because Jesus told him off? The story doesn't tell us. What do you think?

- The faces could be used to recap the story, eg 'What was the name of the man who looked like this at the beginning of the story?', 'Was he a nice polite person?', etc. Children could be asked to copy the faces and imagine the feelings inside them.

- Teach the song. Point out to the children how the third verse fits with the story.

BIBLE BACKGROUND

The story is found in Luke 7:36–50.

I tell you that her many sins are forgiven.
This is clear because she showed great love.
Jesus in Luke 7:47

I CAN MAKE MYSELF BIG

Lively
C F G C F G C F G C F G C F G C F G
I can make my- self big. I can make my- self small. And God puts love in my heart, Be- cause He loves us all.
I can hop on one foot. Now I'm jump- ing on two And God puts love in my heart, So I can do it for you.
I can dance when I'm happy. I can cry when I'm sad And God puts love in my heart, So things won't get too bad.
So clap your hands if you're happy. Clap them if you're O.- K. And God puts love in my heart, Lots of love to- day.

I DON'T HAVE TO DRESS UP TO BE LIKE JESUS

It is what is inside us that counts, not what we look like.

RESOURCES

- The dressing-up box.

CLASS PREPARATION

- Children choose clothes from the dressing-up box and say who they are pretending to be. This might be extended with reasons as to why they would like to be that person.

ASSEMBLY

- Children in dressing-up clothes show the others and say who they are pretending to be.

  It is fun to pretend, but it is best to be you. Who would *Wayne*'s mum like best? *XXX* (whoever *Wayne* was pretending to be) or *Wayne*? Of course, she likes *Wayne* best. That's because *Wayne* is very special and his mum loves him very much. She wouldn't want *XXX* instead!

- **A story: The day Jesus got very cross**

  There was one time when Jesus got very cross with some people who were dressing up. They weren't dressing up like us, though. This was a different sort of dressing up.

  Jesus was in Jerusalem for the special Jewish festival called the Passover. There were thousands and thousands and thousands of other people there, too. You could hardly move with all the visitors who had come specially for the feast.

  And they all wanted to go up to the most holy place of all, the temple. To get there they had to climb up some long, long steps. There were so many people all trying to climb the steps that you were lucky if you could get up just one step in five minutes! You can imagine how long it took to get all the way up to the top.

Now there were some people there called Pharisees. They were very stuck-up sort of people who thought they were much better than everyone else. Jewish men wear prayer shawls when they go to pray, but the Pharisees made their prayer shawls extra long so that everyone would see how holy they were.

Then they stood beside the long, long steps in their long, long prayer shawls and preached long, long sermons. The people had to listen because they were stuck in the crowds moving oh so slowly up the steps. The Pharisees felt very pleased with themselves. They just *loved* people to think how important they were. They loved to hear people call them 'Teacher'. And they loved to have the best seats at parties in the big houses in Jerusalem.

When Jesus saw them he got really cross. He knew that they were just dressing up to show off. They might look like extra good people in their long, long prayer shawls, but inside they were proud and selfish and really rotten.

In front of all the crowds on the long, long steps he gave them a long, long telling-off. He called them all sorts of names. He called them poisonous snakes, and cheats, and said they were like graves full of old bones! He kept on telling them that they were *pretenders* — people who dressed up to pretend how good they were, but really they were so bad inside that God was very angry with them.

We don't want to be like that, do we? We don't want to be pretenders. We don't want just to look good on the outside but be nasty inside.

◆ Sing the song.

Another appropriate song is 'Inside Out'.

BIBLE BACKGROUND

The story is found in Matthew 23:1–35. The steps up to the Temple Mount where the Pharisees preached to the crowds have been excavated and can be visited in Jerusalem today. Several of the references that Jesus makes in this passage are to things that can be seen from these steps.

They make their special prayer clothes very long so that people will notice them.

Matthew 23:5

I DON'T HAVE TO DRESS UP TO BE LIKE JESUS

I HAVE A FRIEND

A classic story, retold to bring in the cultural background and to highlight the shifting emotions.

RESOURCES

- None needed.

ASSEMBLY

◆ **A story: The man with no friends**

'He's coming,' said the women to each other, chattering round the well as they filled their pots with water. 'He's coming here on his way to Jerusalem.'

'He's coming,' said the young men in the shade of a tall palm tree. 'He's going to be made king of the Jews and set us free from the Romans.'

'He's coming,' said the rich merchant, watching his servants with the camels. 'I hope he does beat the Romans. Then I shan't have to pay all my money in taxes.'

'He's coming,' said the Roman officer. 'I'd better have plenty of my soldiers on duty. We don't want any trouble.'

'He's coming,' said the children playing in the street. 'Let's run down the road and be the first to see him.'

The town of Jericho was full of excitement. They were right, he *was* coming. Jesus, that is. He was certain to stop the night in Jericho. That meant he would have to stay at someone's house. There weren't any hotels, you see.

There was such a buzz in the town. They were all wondering if Jesus would do some miracles, and whose house he would stay at, and whether he really was going to be the new king. Everyone was chattering excitedly to each other.

Well, nearly everyone. There was one man who didn't have anyone to chatter to. His name was Zacchaeus, and he was the man with no friends. Zacchaeus was the chief tax collector. His job was to collect money from the merchants who arrived in town with their strings of camels. He collected money from all the people in the town, too. The money was supposed to be sent far away to Rome, but quite a lot of it stayed in Zacchaeus' pockets.

Nobody liked Zacchaeus. The merchants didn't like Zacchaeus because they didn't want to see any of their money go in taxes.

The young men didn't like Zacchaeus because he worked for the Romans. They hated the Romans.

The women didn't like Zacchaeus because they had to scrimp and save and go without when the family paid their taxes.

Zacchaeus walked round Jericho with his nose in the air and pretended not to care. But inside he cared very much. It doesn't matter how rich you are if you haven't any friends. You can have expensive clothes and the best chariot to ride in, but if you are lonely inside, that is just about the worst feeling in the world.

That didn't stop Zacchaeus being interested in Jesus. He had heard many strange and wonderful things about Jesus. He had even heard that Jesus went to parties with tax-collectors! Zacchaeus was really curious to see what sort of person Jesus was.

All at once some of the children came racing down the street. 'He's coming!' they shouted. 'It's Jesus. He'll be here any minute.'

The women put their pots down, the merchant tied his camels up, and the soldiers made themselves look big and fierce. Everyone pushed and shoved to get the best view.

Everyone except Zacchaeus. He was only short, and he was scared of getting hidden in the crowd. If the Roman soldiers couldn't see him, some of the young men might beat him up.

Suddenly he found himself doing the most extraordinary thing. He didn't know what came over him. He started climbing a tree, a big tree hanging over the road.

Now rich people in those days didn't wear trousers. They wore a long robe that came down to their feet and was quite tight around their ankles. The only way Zacchaeus could climb that tree was by pulling his robe up over his knees. And that showed off all his long underpants!

It only took one small boy to shout out, and everyone turned to look up at Zacchaeus. The sight of a pair of long white underpants half way up a tree was the funniest thing people had seen in years! The women put their faces in their hands and giggled helplessly. The young men laughed and shouted out rude things. Even the camels looked surprised and stopped chewing.

Zacchaeus felt so stupid his face turned bright red. Fortunately, just then Jesus and his followers came round the bend in the road. The Roman soldiers gripped their swords. If this Jesus wanted trouble, they were ready to give it to him.

But he didn't look like trouble. He strode up the road, smiling and patting the heads of children. A few people called out, offering him a bed for the night.

Zacchaeus felt better. Everyone had forgotten about him. But then, another extraordinary thing happened. Jesus stopped right underneath that tree and looked straight up at Zacchaeus clinging to a branch.

'Zacchaeus,' he said, 'come down immediately. I must stay at your house today.'

Now Zacchaeus' face turned white. Everyone was looking at him again. He nearly fell out of the tree as he climbed down, but nobody laughed this time. The people had all gone silent. Zacchaeus stumbled up the road with Jesus. He didn't know what to say either.

The rest of the crowd stayed where they were. They had come out to welcome Jesus, but now he had gone off with the man everyone hated. The women got into small groups, muttering to each other. The young men stood with their hands on their hips, looking angry. Jesus could forget about people making him king!

Much later that evening, Jesus and Zacchaeus came out into the market square. People looked at them suspiciously. Zacchaeus seemed to want to say something.

'Er, listen everybody,' he said. 'I've been talking to Jesus and, er, I've told him that I'm going to give half of my money to the poor people in the town.'

Mouths opened in astonishment. People were listening now, all right.

'And another thing,' said Zacchaeus, 'I know you think I've been cheating you. Well, anyone I have cheated, I'm going to pay them back four times more!'

For a moment, the open mouths got wider. Then everybody started talking at once.

Jesus smiled and held up his hand for silence. 'Lots of you thought I was coming to rescue you from the Romans,' he said. 'Well, I have come to rescue people, but not in that way. I've come to rescue people like Zacchaeus, people who are in trouble, people with no friends. Today Zacchaeus has been rescued. He's been rescued from being a cheat, and from being greedy and selfish.

'And now that he has been rescued,' Jesus went on, 'I want you to make friends with him. Because he worked for the Romans, you thought he wasn't part of the family of the Jews. You thought he didn't belong. But he *is* part of the family of the Jews, and now he has proved it. Welcome him back.'

For a moment, nobody moved. Then one man stepped slowly forward and held out his arms to give Zacchaeus a hug. Zacchaeus swallowed hard. Then another man came to hug him, and another. A big tear rolled down Zacchaeus' cheek and fell in the Jericho dust. He wasn't the man with no friends any more.

- Teach the song.

This song is good to dance to. It works well being sung while playing Follow the Leader.

BIBLE BACKGROUND

Salvation has come to this house today. This man truly belongs to the family of Abraham. The Son of Man came to find lost people and save them.

Jesus in Luke 19:9

I HAVE A FRIEND

2. **You have a friend, etc.**
3. **We have a friend, etc.**

I HAVE GOT A STORY TO TELL

Suitable for an Easter service. There was something 'inside' Jesus that was very special.

RESOURCES

- A commercial chocolate Easter egg with sweets inside it.

ASSEMBLY

- Show the children the egg. Everyone enjoys Easter eggs. The chocolate outside is good to eat. And there is something else good hidden away inside it. What is it? Smarties (or whatever).

  Easter is a time when we remember some of the very special things Jesus did. Easter eggs remind us of some of the wonderful things about Jesus.

  The chocolate outside the egg is good. And what people could see of Jesus on the outside was good, too. He taught people how to live good lives. He told them stories that helped them remember important things. He showed he loved people by the way he cared for them.

  But there was something hidden away inside Jesus, like the sweets hidden inside the egg. It was something so special that it often made people ask who Jesus really was. People could see that there was something special inside Jesus because of some of the things he did.

  Sometimes he made sick people better: blind people, lame people, deaf people. (Remind the children of any story they have been told recently.) People said to themselves, 'How can Jesus do this? How can he make sick people better? Who is this Jesus?'

  One time Jesus was in a boat with his followers on the sea of Galilee. A big storm blew up, and the followers thought they were all going to drown. Then Jesus told the storm to calm down. And it did! The followers looked at Jesus in amazement. 'Who is this?' they asked each other. 'Even the wind and the waves do what he tells them to!'

  Another time Jesus made a man walk whose legs were paralysed. He also told the man that all the bad things he had done — his sins — were forgiven. Some of the people who were watching said, 'Only God can forgive sins. Who is this Jesus?'

You see, Jesus was showing people that inside him was something very special, very different, very wonderful. Far more wonderful than a few sweets!

Then on the day we call Good Friday, Jesus was hung on a cross and killed. It was like the shell was broken. People thought that was the end.

But it wasn't the end. Something happened on Easter Sunday that showed Jesus really was different. His friends saw him alive again. They met him and talked to him. It was like now they could really see the special 'inside' Jesus. One day they watched as he was taken up into heaven.

Then they went out and began to tell people all over the world that Jesus was like no one else, that he was the Son of God. And so many people believed them that now we have a holiday at Easter. And we give each other Easter eggs to remind us of Jesus who was very good on the outside. But inside him was something — or someone — very special indeed.

◆ Sing the song.

BIBLE BACKGROUND

The followers were afraid and amazed. They said to each other, 'What kind of man is this?'

Luke 8:25

The Pharisees thought to themselves, 'Who is this man?'

Luke 5:21

I HAVE GOT A STORY TO TELL

Another suggestion would be to split your group up and/or use a marching drum beat.

A

I KNOW THE STORY OF A SPECIAL BABY

When God wants something doing, he sends a baby into the world. Suitable for a Christmas service.

RESOURCES

- Photographs from newspapers and magazines of TV personalities and other people children might know. Include a photo of one of the teachers for extra amusement!

ASSEMBLY

◆ Show the pictures one at a time. Ask the children if they know who it is and what they do. Now ask the children if they can imagine this person as a baby.

As you go through the photographs, suggest amusing mental pictures. For example, can they imagine this person…

- with no hair?
- crying?
- having his nappy changed?
- being bathed in a bowl?
- being showered in talcum-powder?
- needing to be burped?
- playing peep-bo?
- in a baby-bouncer?
- wearing a babygro or bootees, etc.?

◆ It is hard to imagine. But all these people began life as babies. The Prime Minister did not come into the world wearing a suit and able to give long speeches! He (or she) wore baby clothes and had to learn to talk just like everyone else.

It seems that when God wants something doing, he sends a baby into the world.

In lots of countries all over the world at Christmas, people celebrate the birth of a special baby. (All babies are special, but this one was *very* special.) Whose birthday do people celebrate at Christmas? Jesus. They celebrate his birth because he grew up to become the most famous person in the world.

- This might be a moment for retelling the Christmas story, or recapping it by asking the children questions.
- Teach the song. It's likely to become a firm favourite!

Emphasise the wonder of God using the most unlikely things. He can use us, too!

A further suitable song is 'God Gave Noah a Job to Do' — God gave Mary a job to do, Joseph, Jesus, the shepherds, etc.

BIBLE BACKGROUND

You will give birth to a son and you will name him Jesus. He will be great, and people will call him the Son of the Most High.

The angel Gabriel to Mary in Luke 1:31–32

I KNOW THE STORY OF A SPECIAL BABY.

IF YOU GRUMBLE OR COMPLAIN

*This assembly can stand on its own, or be the introduction to a No Moaning or Arguing week. This will require the co-operation of all the staff. The follow-up assembly, **I SEE A STAR**, rewards those who have made a special effort during the week.*

RESOURCES

- None needed.

ASSEMBLY

- Who has had a grumble or a moan or a complain today? Most of us have something to grumble about. Teachers usually have lots to grumble about! It's OK to do a bit of grumbling now and then, but no one likes someone who grumbles all the time.

  This is a story about a person called Alfred Dumble. When he was a boy, Alfred moaned about *everything*. Nothing was ever right for him. When he grew up and got married, he wasn't any better. How his poor wife coped, nobody knew. Then one day, a black cloud came and settled right over his head. Listen to what happened.

The Tale of Alfred Dumble

Here's the sad tale of Alfred Dumble
Who found life one long pain.
He only opened his mouth to grumble
And mutter and complain.

One Christmas time young Alfred Dumble
Received a brand-new bike.
He moaned, 'It's only fit for jumble —
It's not the kind I like.'

His teacher said, 'Please, Alfred Dumble,
It isn't nice to moan.
If all you ever do is grumble
You'll get left on your own.'

But did he try? Not Alfred Dumble,
  It just was not his style.
It seemed he couldn't be that humble
  To say 'sorry' with a smile.

Whatever she did for Alfred Dumble,
  His wife could never win.
She made a scrumptious apple crumble —
  He threw it in the bin!

Then in the air over Alfred Dumble
  A cloud was seen to grow.
Big drops of rain began to tumble,
  And showers began to flow.

That cloud seemed stuck to Alfred Dumble,
  It never left his head.
It rained while in the dark he fumbled,
  It rained on him in bed!

When he went out poor Alfred Dumble
  Made people stop and stare.
They heard the sound of thunder rumble,
  Saw lightning in his hair!

So all the more did Alfred Dumble
  Have reason to complain,
As 'neath his private cloud he stumbled
  In his private shower of rain.

Now please don't be like Alfred Dumble,
  And whinge and moan and whine.
On those who only live to grumble
  The sun will never shine.

◆ Poor Alfred Dumble! Do you think he got what he deserved?

A long time ago a man called Paul wrote lots of letters which are in the Bible. One of the things he wrote was to tell people to 'do everything without complaining or arguing'. Here is what he said:

Do everything without complaining or arguing. Then you will be innocent and without anything wrong in you. You will be God's children without fault. But

you are living with crooked and mean people all around you. Among them you shine like stars in the dark world.

What a lovely picture! Paul said that people who do everything without complaining or arguing are like stars shining in a dark world. It's much nicer to be a star than to walk around with your own black cloud like Alfred Dumble!

Let's have a No Moaning or Arguing week. We'll all see if we can make a special effort not to moan or complain or argue this week. Then next week we'll see who are the 'stars', the people who usually have a bit of a moan but have been much more smiley people than usual.

- Teach the song. This song should help us remember not to be like Alfred Dumble.
- Ask staff to note children who make a special effort not to grumble or complain this week. This is a way of reminding and encouraging those who habitually moan and argue rather than rewarding those who are of a naturally sunny disposition.

BIBLE BACKGROUND

The quotation is from the Apostle Paul in Philippians 2:14–15.

IF YOU GRUMBLE OR COMPLAIN

I SEE A STAR

This is the follow-up to 'If You Grumble or Complain'. It rewards those who have worked hard at displaying a more positive attitude.

RESOURCES

- Some silver stars, either large ones to hold, or made as badges. Ask staff for names of children to commend for their efforts in not complaining or arguing during the past week.

ASSEMBLY

- Start with a rerun of last week's assembly. Read the story of Alfred Dumble again, and Paul's words from the letter to the Philippians.
- Teach the song, 'I See a Star'.
- Bring the children who have been named to the front one at a time. Relate any details about how they managed to smile and be nice instead of complaining or arguing. Give them a star. Commend them as examples for others to copy. Sing the song to them.

  Repeat for each child.

BIBLE BACKGROUND

Those who teach others to live right will shine like stars for ever and ever.

Daniel 12:3

This song can also be used when a child has done something especially good. The child stands up and the class sings the song to them.

IF YOU KNOW THAT JESUS LOVES YOU CLAP YOUR HANDS

A simple assembly, good for the end of the day, and for reinforcing good behaviour and attitudes.

RESOURCES

- None needed.

ASSEMBLY

- Ask the children to do an action if they have done certain things such as those listed below. Actions could be: nod your head, wave your hand, rub your tummy, scratch your nose, etc. Stress the need to think about whether they really have done these things. No cheating! Individuals can be asked what it is they have done.

  Here are some suggestions:

  - if you've been a good friend
  - helped someone
  - tidied up
  - learnt something new
  - told your mum you love her
  - put rubbish in the bin
  - run an errand for someone
  - told the truth when you nearly told a lie
  - said sorry for something.

- All these are good things to do. And when we *do* something good, it makes us *feel* good inside.

  Another thing that makes people feel good is knowing that Jesus loves them. Jesus loves us all the time, whether we do good things or bad things. But Jesus is sad when we do silly things. And he is happy when we do good things.

Sing the song.

◆ **More...**

The song can be used in conjunction with the story of Palm Sunday. Verses can include: 'Wave your arms'; 'shout hurrah!'

BIBLE BACKGROUND

My children, our love should not be only words and talk.
Our love must be true love. And we should show that love by what we do.

The Apostle John in 1 John 3:18

IF YOU KNOW THAT JESUS LOVES YOU

You can add whatever actions you feel are appropriate.
Some suggestions are:-

Wave your arms
Stamp your feet
Say 'We do!'
Turn around
Nod your head

IF YOU WANT TO WORK FOR JESUS

Learning to be kind and caring, but realising that sometimes we need help.

RESOURCES

- Anything that works with batteries — radio, torch, toys, cassette player. Try to get at least one with moving parts.
- You could have a piece of liver from the butcher's to show.

ASSEMBLY

- Show your battery-operated items and demonstrate. They each need energy, or power, to make them work. Where does the energy come from? From the batteries inside. Energy is stored inside the batteries. Wires or strips of metal inside the torch or toy carry the energy to where it is needed. When the batteries run down, you have to buy new ones. You can also get some special batteries that you can recharge. Recharging fills them up with energy so you can use them again.
- Choose a lively child and get him to jump up and down. Where does his energy come from? Does *Darren*'s mum charge his batteries before he comes to school in the morning? Of course not!

  But *Darren*'s body still has to store energy. The place it stores energy is called his liver. (Show the animal liver, if you have it.) *Darren*'s liver is right in the middle of his body. It is a bit like a great big battery. It stores energy and then sends it in *Darren*'s blood to his muscles. That is how he gets the energy to jump up and down and run around and play football.

  When *Darren* gets tired and runs out of energy, his mum doesn't take his liver out and change it! But she does make sure he has his breakfast, and his dinner, and his tea. That's where his energy comes from in the first place, from the food he has to eat. The food recharges his liver, and then he is ready to come out and play again. Isn't that clever!
- There is something else *Darren* needs when he is playing. We all do. We need to be able to play without fighting. We need to be able to play without being unkind to people, or being selfish, or saying nasty things to people. That can be hard. Sometimes we start by being quite sure we are going to be good and not get into trouble, then it's as if our batteries run down and we do some-

thing silly. Is there some way we can stop our 'goodness batteries' from running out?

Here is a true story about a man who got into lots of trouble, very serious trouble, and how he got new 'goodness batteries'. His name is David Lant.

◆ **David Lant's story**

David first got into trouble with the police when he was only eight years old. After that it seemed as though there was nothing left in his 'goodness batteries' at all. He was always fighting, and hurting people, and stealing things. He had to be locked up in places for young people who got into bad trouble. Every time he came out, he started doing bad things again. This went on for twenty years.

Then he committed a crime so serious that he was sent to prison for a long, long time. People said he was one of the most dangerous men in prison in England.

One day he took part in a television programme about men in prison. A lady called Margaret saw the programme and wrote him a letter. She said she was a Christian and that she was praying for him. David wasn't interested in that. He didn't believe in God.

A little while later, David was alone in his cell one night. He started thinking about all the things he had done. He did not like himself. He wanted to stop hurting people. He wanted to be different, but he knew he could not change his 'goodness batteries' himself. He needed someone to help him. He needed someone to love him.

He got down on his knees and started praying, talking to God. He said sorry for all the bad things he had done. He asked God to help him change into a better person.

Two weeks later David woke up in the middle of the night and started whistling a tune. He didn't know what it was, but he went on whistling it all morning. Then at dinnertime, another prisoner got out a hymnbook and showed David the words to the tune he was whistling. It was a song all about God forgiving even the worst person. David knew that God had heard his prayer.

From then on, he started to become a different person. He is still in prison, but now he is a very caring person. He has decided to spend his life helping other people. He does this by making books for blind people. David uses a computer to translate words into Braille, the special language made of bumps on a page that blind people can read with their fingers. David's Braille books go all over the world, in all sorts of languages.* He has even won a prize for helping people.

---

* David Lant's Braille ministry operates as part of LIGHTWING PROJECTS, Registered Charity no. 1016529. For his full story, and other details, see the website at http://www.wyrecompute.oaktree.co.uk/lightwing.

- That is a true story about how one person got new 'goodness batteries'. Of course, it is much better to get our 'goodness batteries' recharged every day and not get into big, big trouble like David did. David got his batteries changed when he prayed to God. We can do the same.

- **A prayer**

  Father God, we don't want to do bad things and get into trouble. Please recharge our 'goodness batteries' and help us to be kind and caring. Amen.

- Teach the song.

BIBLE BACKGROUND

With God's power working in us, God can do much, much more than anything we can ask or think of.

The Apostle Paul in Ephesians 3:20

IF YOU WANT TO WORK FOR JESUS

C (P)

I'LL REMEMBER

Memories are important.

RESOURCES

- Personal souvenirs, photos, things saved from childhood.
- Either a cross or a Remembrance Day poppy (a large one could be made to display).

CLASS PREPARATION (Optional)

- Children could bring items of their own from home to talk about, eg photos of when they were small, a shell brought back from a seaside holiday, a present from a grandparent.

ASSEMBLY

◆ Remembering things that happened in the past is very important. Who has photos at home of when they were small? Scrapbooks? Home videos? Who has shells or pebbles or things brought back from holiday?

Either show some of your own mementoes or use a group of children who have prepared to show theirs.

These are things that are special to us because they remind us of things that have happened in our lives that are important to us. Or they remind us of people who are special to us.

◆ There are other things that remind lots of people of things that are important to them.

Show and talk about one or more of the following.

- **A cross.** Ask children if they can remember seeing a cross on a local church building and can say where it is. Some people wear a cross on a chain around their neck.

  The cross is important to Christians because it reminds them about how Jesus died. Roman soldiers nailed him to a wooden cross and left him to die. It was very slow and painful. Christians remember that it says in the

Bible that Jesus died to save them. It makes them sad when they think about Jesus dying, but they also want to say thank you.

There is a famous hymn about Jesus dying on the cross. One of the verses goes like this:

> He died that we might be forgiven,
> He died to make us good,
> That we might go at last to heaven,
> Saved by his precious blood.
>
> ('There is a green hill far away',
> Cecil Frances Alexander [1818-95], v. 3)

- **A poppy as used for Remembrance Sunday.** Poppies are used on Remembrance Day to remind us of all the soldiers who have been killed or wounded fighting in wars. There was a war called the Great War, or the First World War, at the time of your great-great-grandfathers. Many, many soldiers died in that war. In the places where they died, a lot of red poppies grew in the spring.* For the soldiers who came back from the war, when they saw poppies it reminded them of their friends who had died in the battles.

  Even though most of us do not have friends or relatives who have died in wars, we wear poppies to help us remember the soldiers who gave their lives to protect our country from enemies. The money we give goes to help old soldiers who are still alive.

◆ Sing the song.

◆ **More...**

A further alternative is to borrow a Communion chalice from a local church and to talk about how bread and wine are used in the Eucharist, or Communion, to remember the death of Jesus. In 1 Corinthians 11:24, Paul records the words of Jesus at the Last Supper: 'Do this to remember me.'

BIBLE BACKGROUND

In the future your children will ask you, 'What do these rocks mean?' Tell them.

Joshua 4:21–22

* Poppies typically grow on disturbed ground, hence their prevalence in the trenches and shell-holes of First World War battlefields.

I'LL REMEMBER

Split your group of children appropriately or have your group of children repeat the echo quietly.

Alternatively, the leader could be the 1st voice and the children the echo.

I'M NOT AN ACCIDENT

It is not uncommon for children to overhear their parents saying that they were 'an accident'. This song was written to put in something more positive. It has also proved popular with children with special needs.

RESOURCES

- The ultrasound scan picture of a baby on page 180 (photocopied on to OHP acetate for best effect with a large group).

ASSEMBLY

- If an everyday accident has occurred in school in the past day or two, talk about that. Otherwise talk about simple accidents like a glass of orange being spilt, or something being dropped and broken.

  Sometimes when an accident happens we can stick the pieces back together, but usually they get thrown away. The spilt orange gets mopped up and we have a fresh glass. That's what accidents are like: things get broken and wasted.

  Can people be accidents? No! They can *have* accidents, but they can't *be* accidents.

  Choose a child to come to the front.

  Is *Emma* an accident? No! Look at her. Look at her lovely face. See where her eyes are, right high up. That's so she can see where she is going easily. It wouldn't be any good if she had her eyes on her knees, would it! What would happen? *Emma* would keep bumping into things. It's not an accident that *Emma*'s eyes are high up on her head.

  Look at her nose. That's high up, too. What do we use our noses for? Breathing. If *Emma* goes swimming she needs her nose and mouth high up to keep them out of the water. What would happen if *Emma* had her nose in the middle of her tummy? She would drown! *Emma*'s nose isn't an accident.

  And look at *Emma*'s mouth. As well as breathing, what does she use it for? Eating. *Emma*'s mouth is close to her eyes so she can see what she is about to put in her mouth and make sure she doesn't eat something nasty. And it's close to her nose where she can smell the food before she puts it in her mouth.

That way she knows if something is bad before she eats it and makes herself poorly. *Emma*'s mouth isn't an accident.

In fact, none of *Emma* is an accident. Every part of her is just right. Every part is in the right place to do the right job. *Emma* isn't an accident. Nobody is an accident.

◆ Sometimes accidents happen *to* people. Some people can't move their arms or legs very well because they couldn't breathe properly when they were born.

For some other people, an accident has happened to their genes, the tiny instructions that tell a baby how to grow inside its mummy. That means they might have to work very hard to do things most of us do easily, or even not be able to do some things at all.

That is not because they *are* an accident. It is because an accident has happened to them.

◆ Show the ultrasound scan picture of an unborn baby. Ask the children if they know what it is. This baby had been growing inside its mummy's tummy for twenty weeks when this picture was taken. We can't see here, but it turned out to be a boy.

What bits of him can you see? His head... his nose... one ear... etc. He is all being put together inside his mummy with all the bits of his body in the right place. Just like us. He's not an accident. Nobody is an accident.

There is a poem in the Bible about this. The man who wrote the poem is talking to God. He says:

> **I praise you because you made me in an amazing and wonderful way.**
> **What you have done is wonderful. I know this very well.**
> **You saw my bones being formed as I took shape in my mother's body.**
> **When I was put together there, you saw my body as it was formed.**
> **All the days planned for me were written in your book before I was one day old.**
>
> **Psalm 139:14–16**

The person who wrote that poem wanted to say thank you to God for making him. He knew he wasn't an accident. He was sure God had planned him and knew all about him. That is true for everyone.

Let's learn one of the lines of the poem and say it together:

> **I praise you because you made me in an amazing and wonderful way.**

◆ Sing the song.

◆ **More...**

For a follow-up assembly, especially a class assembly, involve the children in thinking of verses for a poem based on Psalm 139.

Teach this chorus first:

Now isn't it funny,
That in my mummy's tummy,
Every bit of me took shape.

Ask the children to name bits of the body. See if together they can come up with pairs of words that start with the same sound, eg **toes and tums**.

Put these together in verses like this:

Hair and heads
And cheeks and chin,
God made me wonderfully well.

Other suggested pairs: ears and eyes; neck and nails; feet and fingers; knees and nose; bottoms and bellybuttons; bones and blood; teeth and tongue; hands and hearts.

BIBLE BACKGROUND

In Christ, he chose us before the world was made.
The Apostle Paul in Ephesians 1:4

I'M NOT AN ACCIDENT
Slowly with feeling
D
A Sus 4
Ooo
Ooo
E Min
D
Ooo
Ooo
A Sus 4
G
Ooo- oo- oo
I'm not an
I might be
D
E Min
G
acc- i- dent because my life was meant to be - -
dif- fe- rent but my life was meant to be - -
A
D
E Min
I'm not an acc- i- dent because I'm hea- ven sent to
I might be dif- fe- rent but I'm quite con- tent to
G
A
3
G
be - - the per- son you see
be - - the per- son you see.

I'M WALKING ALONG THE ROAD

The actions to accompany this Bible story help children to empathise with the people involved, almost literally stepping into their shoes.

RESOURCES

- Space for some children to do the actions while the story is told.

ASSEMBLY

- When we come into the hall or our classroom, we try to come in walking sensibly. When we go out in the playground, we often run or skip. There are lots of ways of walking: big steps or small steps, quickly or slowly, steadily or skipping.

  This is a story about what happened one day in a small town when Jesus came. In this story, there are people who walk in all kinds of different ways. As we listen to the story, some children are going to show us how different people in the story were walking.

- **A story: The man who danced in the street**

  It was just an ordinary day in a small town in Galilee. The sun was hot, as usual. Farmers were sitting on the ground selling vegetables, as usual. Children were learning their lessons in the synagogue school, as usual. The synagogue was the Jewish place of worship, but it was also where children were taught to read and learn God's laws off by heart. Their teacher was called a *rabbi*.

  At the end of lessons, the children were eager to stretch their legs, just like you. Off they went into the street, skipping and jumping.

  Let's have one or two people to come out and jump and skip like the Jewish children in the story.

  I expect they got shouted at to be careful, just like you do sometimes. As well as the farmers sitting on the ground with their vegetables, there were mums walking along with pots of water on their heads.

  Let's have someone show us how to walk as if they had a heavy pot of water on their head. You have to stand very straight, and walk slowly and steadily.

Then the people heard some shouting and the sound of a horse's hooves. It was some Roman soldiers coming through the town. Their officer was riding on a horse. Mums pulled their children into doorways, and everyone got out of the way.

Let's see if someone can show us how a horse walks. It picks its front legs up high — clip, clop, clip, clop.

And now we want someone to march like a soldier: head up, big strides, arms swinging.

When the soldiers had gone, everyone came back out into the street, and life went on as usual. But not for long. 'Look! It's that man Jesus,' shouted some-one, 'the rabbi who lives in Capernaum. He's the one who has been making sick people better.' At once people started running to see.

Let's have someone running, leaning forward because you are excited and want to see what is going on.

Soon there was quite a crowd gathered round Jesus. Then another man came into sight down the empty end of the street. He wasn't running or skipping or jumping. He couldn't. He had a nasty skin disease, leprosy. When he walked, he could only hobble.

Let's have someone hobble along slowly, like the man with leprosy.

Some of the people saw him coming. They were frightened of leprosy. It was a terrible disease, and there was no cure. They started backing away, not wanting the man with the leprosy to come near them.

Let's have a person who is good at pretending. You have to imagine you are really scared, and step backwards slowly.

But Jesus wasn't scared. He let the man with leprosy come right up to him. The man bowed before Jesus and begged him, 'Lord, heal me. I know you can if you want to.'

Jesus said, 'I want to. Be healed!' As he said it, Jesus touched him. People in the crowd gasped. They would never, ever touch a leper.

But those who were still close enough to see gasped for a different reason. The nasty white patches on the man's face and hands had gone. Instead, there was just nice pinky-brown skin.

'Go and show yourself to the priest,' said Jesus. 'He will check you out so that people will know you are really better. And take a gift with you to say thank you to God.'

The man went off down the road. He wasn't walking. He wasn't even running. He was so happy he was dancing down the road! He was off to the priest as fast as he could to prove that he was healed.

Let's have one last person who can show us what it's like to dance when you are really happy.

- Teach the song. For a class assembly with enough space, everyone could move appropriately to accompany the song.

BIBLE BACKGROUND

The story is found in Luke 5:12–16.

Jesus touched the man. Immediately the disease disappeared.

Luke 5:13

I AM WALKING ALONG THE ROAD

I am marching
I am hopping
I am running
I am clapping
I am dancing
I am praising
I am praying
I am crying
I am jumping

Choose whatever action/s might be suitable for your own group.

INCY WINCY SPIDER

Understanding why we can't see God.

RESOURCES

- A spider made from wool hung on a thin or 'invisible' thread, or a picture of a real spider.
- Some perfume.

ASSEMBLY

◆ Show the wool 'spider' or the picture. Talk about spiders. Lots of people find spiders scary, but they are good friends because they catch flies and other insects. One of the most fascinating things you can do is to watch a garden spider spinning its web. This is one of the wonders of the world.

A spider's thread comes out of its bottom. The spider squeezes it out. If you can imagine glue coming out of a tube and setting straight away, it's a bit like that. Spiders make two sorts of threads. One sort is sticky, so that when an insect flies into it, it can't get away. The other sort is not sticky. The spider only walks on the threads that aren't sticky, otherwise she would get stuck herself. Isn't that clever!

Spiders' threads are so fine you often can't see them. You know the thread is there because the spider is hanging in mid-air. Who has ever picked a spider up by its thread?

There are lots of other things we can't see, but we know they are there. Here are some.

- Warmth. Rub your hands together. Now put them on your cheeks. What do you feel? Warmth. We can't see it, but we can feel it.
- Perfume. Sprinkle a little so that children can smell it. We can't see it, but we know it's there because it smells nice.
- TV signals. They are all around us, but we can't see them, or hear them, or feel them, or smell them. We know they are there because when we switch on our TV sets we get sound and pictures.

- Some people say they don't believe in God because they can't see him. Other people say they do believe in God because they see the things he has made, or because they feel his love.

  One of Jesus' friends said this:

  > **No man has ever seen God, but [Jesus] is very close to the Father. And [Jesus] has shown us what God is like.**

  The world is full of things we can't see, like warmth or perfume or TV signals or spiders' threads. But we have lots of ways of knowing they are there. Jesus' friends said he was one of the best ways of knowing that God is there and discovering what he is like.

- If you have a wool spider, choose a child to dance the spider on its thread. Sing the song.

BIBLE BACKGROUND

No man has ever seen God, but God the only Son is very close to the Father. And the Son has shown us what God is like.

The Apostle John in John 1:18

For more on the same theme, see **JESUS IS THERE, THERE, THERE.**

INCY WINCY SPIDER

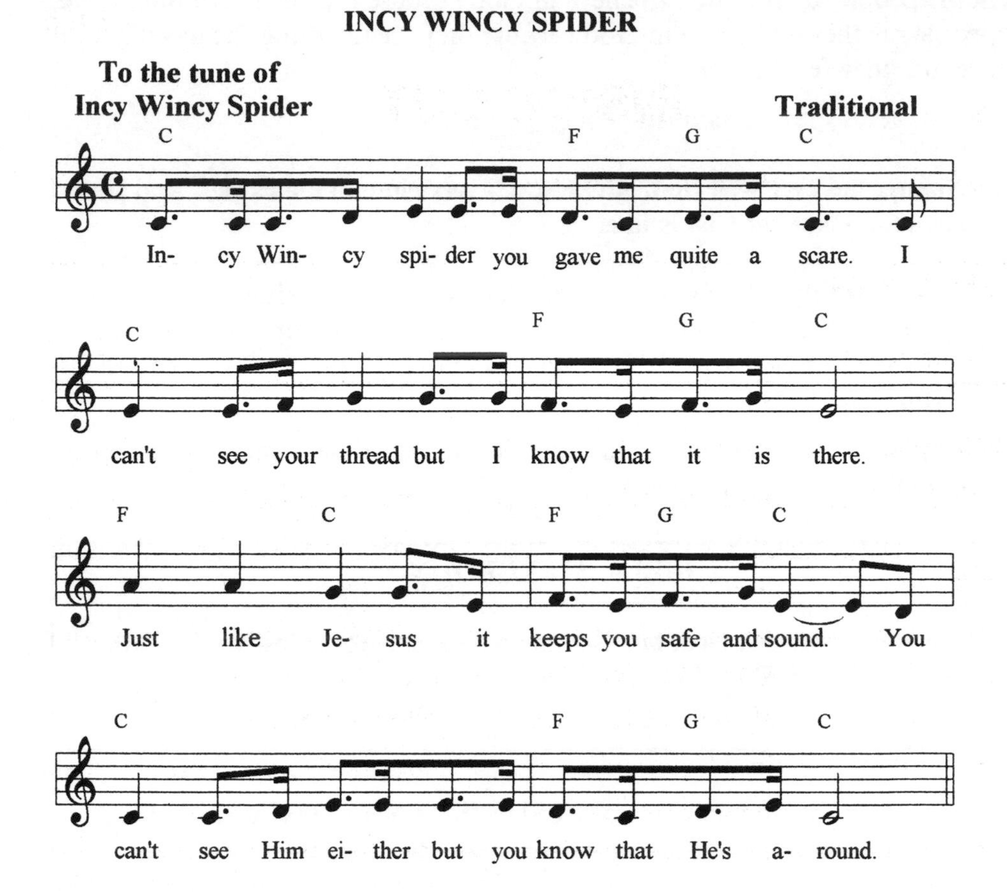

Get the children to pretend they are holding a spider on a thread. Pass the spider from one finger and thumb to another as you sing.

A T C S

INSIDE OUT

Thinking good thoughts and turning them into actions.

RESOURCES

- None needed.

ASSEMBLY

◆ What goes on in our heads when we have our mouths closed? *Thinking.*

When we do something it starts as a thought inside our heads. Then our brain tells our hands or our legs or our mouths what to do.

We are going to ask some people to do some thinking for us. Then we are going to try to guess what they are thinking.

Choose a couple of children to do each of the following.

- Think of a feeling. Now make a face to show the feeling. Who can guess what feeling *Philip* is thinking about?
- Think of something we do in school every day. Now act it — show us how you do it. Who can guess what thing we do in school *Caroline* is thinking about?
- Think of an animal. Now act it — show us what the animal looks like or how it moves. Who can guess what animal *Alex* is thinking about?

◆ Now it is everybody's turn to do some thinking. Think of something you can do today to make someone else happy. It might be something helpful. It might be a job that needs doing. It might be saying something nice to someone. It might be making friends with someone. Has everyone thought of something? (Some children might be asked what they have thought of.)

The next thing is to make sure you do it. It would have been no good if the animal *Alex* thought of was a *lion* but he did nothing to show us. Think first, then do it.

◆ Followers of Jesus believe God works inside people if they let him. He works deep, deep in their hearts to help them think good thoughts, kind thoughts, helpful thoughts. Then he helps them to do it.

- **A prayer**

  Father God, help me to think good thoughts today. Help me not to keep the thoughts inside me but to turn them into good actions. Amen.

- Sing the song, with the actions.

BIBLE BACKGROUND

Yes, God is working in you to help you want to do what pleases him.
Then he gives you the power to do it.

The Apostle Paul in Philippians 2:13

For more on similar themes see **WE DON'T HAVE TO DRESS UP** and **I CAN MAKE MYSELF BIG**.

INSIDE OUT

To the tune of This Old Man **Traditional**

I'VE GOT SOMETHING VERY SPECIAL

Things that are special to individuals, and the special love that is there for everyone.

RESOURCES

- Small objects of value, sentimental or otherwise, that staff can bring in. (Can also work with pretend objects.)

ASSEMBLY

- Members of staff take it in turns to hold something hidden in their hand or behind their back and say, 'I've got something very special and it belongs to me. Can you guess what it is?' Give clues as necessary until someone guesses. One should be a wedding or engagement ring. Other suggestions:
  - locket with photo, or other piece of jewellery
  - stone or shell from holiday
  - memento of childhood
  - lock of baby's hair/baby's first shoe
  - telephone number or address of someone special
  - a letter or thank-you note
  - a picture drawn by a grandchild.
- Now tell the children that you have something special, but this time it is invisible. You can't see it, you can't hold it, you can't keep it in a drawer or hang it on the wall. Can anyone guess what it is? A clue: it has something to do with the wedding ring. Answer: love.
- We all have someone who loves us — mums and dads, grans and granddads, brothers and sisters, friends.

  The Bible says there is someone who loves everyone — and his love is the best love of all. That's Jesus. You can't see Jesus' love; you can't hold it in your hand or keep it in a box of treasures. Yet it's the best treasure of all. And it is for every single person in the world.
- Sing the song.

BIBLE BACKGROUND

This is how God showed his love to us: he sent his only Son into the world to give us life through him.

The Apostle John in 1 John 4:9

I'VE GOT SOMETHING VERY SPECIAL

JESUS AND GOD GO TOGETHER

This song is good for developing rhythm and motor skills. It is also good for classifying. It can be used for points that teachers want to emphasise, such as family relationships or whatever is topical.

RESOURCES

- None needed.

ASSEMBLY

- Teach the chorus first, including the actions.

  Sing a couple of appropriate verses and choruses, then ask the children for suggestions for other verses.

- **A thought: Doing things together**

  Fathers and sons go together. So do mothers and sons, and fathers and daughters, and mothers and daughters. They love each other and like doing things together. They share things and show each other things. They laugh together at things that are funny and cry together when there is something sad.

  Of course, every father is different, and every mother is different. Every son is different, and every daughter is different. So the things they do together are different for every family. It might be playing together, or going to a football match together, or watching a favourite TV programme together, or going shopping together.

  Give some examples from your own family, or things that you know some of the children do with their parents.

  The song says Jesus and God go together. Jesus called God his Father. He called himself the Son. Do you learn things from watching your parents? Jesus did, too. He said he only did what he saw his Father doing. Another time he said that he only spoke the words his Father taught him to speak. It's good to learn from our parents, isn't it?

  Jesus was telling his followers that he and God belonged together, that they were very close. They loved each other and did things together, just like we do with our parents.

BIBLE BACKGROUND

The Father and I are one.
Jesus in John 10:30

JESUS AND GOD GO TOGETHER

Other suggestions:

Butter and Bread
Fish and Chips
Mums and Dads
Hands and Fingers

Reinforce the message by repeating the first verse alternately.

JESUS HELPED HIS DAD TO MAKE THE WORLD

Learning about the water cycle and how every part of creation has its vital place.

RESOURCES

- Paper and paints.

CLASS PREPARATION

- Teach about the water cycle. Extend it to include plants, which need water to grow, animals, who need water to drink and plants to eat, and people, who also need water to drink and plants to eat.

  Cut out large jigsaw-shaped pieces of paper. Get children to paint one of the following on each: sea, sun, wind, clouds, rain, rivers, plants, animals, people.

ASSEMBLY

- Children present their pictures one at a time and talk about them (with help as necessary).
  - The sea. The sea is enormous and contains lots of water. But the water is salty and you can't drink it.
  - The sun. Hot sun shines on the sea and the land. What happens when the sun shines on a puddle? It dries up. The water seems to disappear, but really it goes into the air. We say it *evaporates*. The sun makes water evaporate from the sea.
  - The wind. When the wind blows, it helps water evaporate. That's why mum's washing dries quickly on the line on a windy day.
  - Clouds. The water in the air makes tiny droplets. Then it isn't invisible any more. We can see it in the sky as clouds. Clouds are mountains of tiny drops of water in the sky.
  - Rain. The tiny drops of water in the clouds get bigger and bigger until they start to fall out of the sky. They fall as rain.

- Rivers. Some of the rain makes streams and rivers and runs back into the sea.
- Plants. Some of the rain soaks into the ground. Plants grow. Plants need lots of water to grow. In the deserts, where there is not much rain, not many plants grow.
- Animals. Lots of animals eat plants. We all know how much a rabbit likes nice fresh cabbage leaves or a carrot. Animals need to drink water, too. In the wild, they drink from ponds and streams.
- People. People are a kind of animal. We need food and water, just like the other animals. We eat plants and meat from animals. Most of the water we drink comes out of the tap. The water companies get the water from rivers, or collect it in big lakes called reservoirs.

◆ Sea, sun, wind, clouds, rain, rivers, plants, animals, people — we are all part of a big jigsaw. All the pieces fit together. It is a very clever jigsaw. If just one of the parts of the jigsaw was missing, we would not be here. There would be no people on the Earth. There would be no *Anytown School*, no clever people to paint pictures.

In the Bible, it tells us how God made the world. It says that Jesus was there, too, helping God. God wanted a planet where people could live. He wanted to make a place where they could grow, and learn about him, and love each other.

So God and Jesus made the world. Actually, there are lots more pieces in the jigsaw of the world than we have here — millions of pieces, billions of pieces! Every plant, every animal, every person is a piece in God's jigsaw. Each one of us is a piece in God's jigsaw. If you weren't here, there would be a hole in God's jigsaw! God would be unhappy. His jigsaw would not be complete without you.

◆ Teach the song.

BIBLE BACKGROUND

Before the world began, there was the Word. The Word was with God, and the Word was God. He was with God in the beginning. All things were made through him. Nothing was made without him.

The Apostle John, introducing Jesus in John 1:1–3

JESUS HELPED HIS DAD TO MAKE THE WORLD

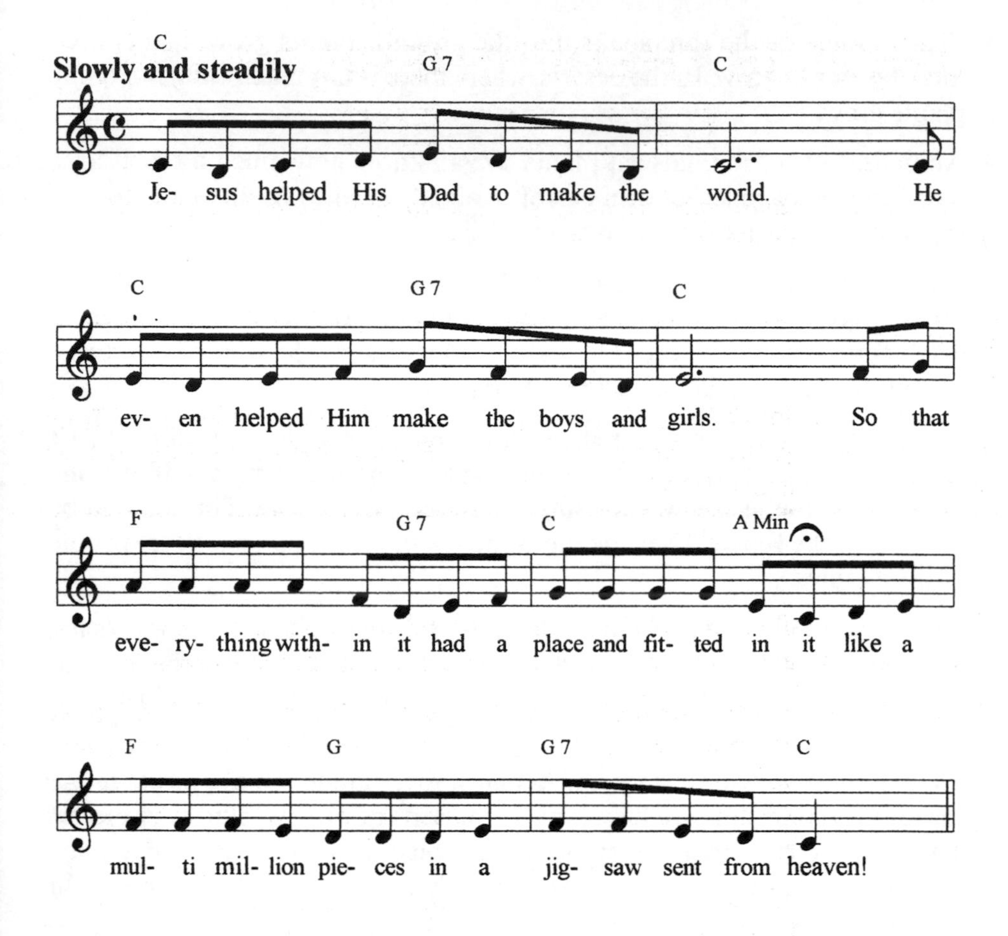

JESUS IS THERE, THERE, THERE, THERE, THERE

Thinking about air and static electricity helps us to appreciate the reality of other things we can't see.

RESOURCES

- Two inflated balloons (plus a spare) of different colours; clothing made from nylon or other synthetic fabric; a large table. Practise beforehand (see below) so you know that the 'trick' works.

ASSEMBLY

- What does 'invisible' mean? If something is invisible, does that mean it is not there at all? We are going to think about some things that are invisible.

  - The first one is easy to think about: air. Air is all around us, though we can't see it. Everybody take a deep breath. Can you feel the air going into your nose or your mouth? Now blow on your hands. It is easy to feel air when we blow it on our hands. We can't see air, but we can feel it so we know it's there.

    When air outside is moving, we call that wind. Wind is like breath. How do we know it's there? We can feel it. We can also see leaves moving, or bits of litter blowing around. If the wind is blowing strongly, we can hear the noise it makes.

  - The second invisible thing is much more strange, although it is all around us, just like air. We can use it to make a balloon do a magic trick.

    Rub one balloon on clothing and place it on the table (or floor, if every child can see). Rub the second balloon similarly. Hold it and move it close to the first balloon. The first balloon should move away when the second comes within a few centimetres. Make sure the children can see that the balloons are not touching. Explain what is happening.

    When the *red* balloon comes near the *white* balloon, the *white* balloon moves away. It looks like magic. It is really science magic. Something is making the *white* balloon move without touching it. It isn't air blowing it. It is electricity. Electricity is what makes lights work, and TVs, and kettles, and computers. But we have to plug those in. We didn't plug the balloon in, did we? This is a special sort of electricity. It is called static electricity. That means it doesn't move, it stays in one place. You can make static electricity on a balloon by rubbing it on your jumper. The static electricity on one balloon pushes against the static electricity on the other balloon so strongly that it makes the second balloon roll away.

Another trick that sometimes works is to rub a balloon and hold it against a wall. The balloon sticks to the wall. This time the static electricity is acting like invisible glue, stopping the balloon falling down.

If you rub a balloon and hold it close to your face, you feel something strange. It is just a little tickly feeling. That is the static electricity pulling the tiny little hairs on your face. You can feel the hairs standing up.

Static electricity is around us all the time. Sometimes in winter, on a cold frosty day, if you take your clothes off in the dark you see tiny sparks. That is static electricity, too.

- So there are two invisible things, air and static electricity. Here is another. When Jesus went back to heaven, he made a promise to his friends. He said, 'You can be sure that I will be with you always. I will continue with you until the end of the world.'

  Lots of people all over the world think of Jesus as their invisible friend. They can't see him, but they know he is there. They know he listens when they talk to him. They feel his love around them.

- Teach the song.

BIBLE BACKGROUND

**You can be sure that I will be with you always.
I will continue with you until the end of the world.**

Jesus in Matthew 28:20

For more on the same theme, see **INCY WINCY SPIDER**.

JESUS IS THERE

C

LIFE IS A BEAUTIFUL THING, YOU KNOW

You don't need to look further than out of a suburban office window to find a love story to tell. This one will exercise children's imagination and teach them something about real life. As Jesus said, 'Look at the birds of the air.'

RESOURCES

- None needed.

ASSEMBLY

◆ **A true love story**

Mr and Mrs Wood Pigeon are sitting on a long curved branch in the old silver birch tree in the garden.

You could paint Mr and Mrs Wood Pigeon very easily if you wanted to. First get a lot of white paint and mix in just enough black to make a grey the same colour as clay. That will be just right for their wings and backs and heads. Then mix an extra bit of black in to make the end of their square tails a little darker. Now get some more white and mix in just a tiny bit of black and a tiny bit of red. When you have a pinky-grey colour, that will be perfect for their big fat chests.

There is one more important thing if you are going to paint Mr and Mrs Wood Pigeon: you have to give them a smart white collar on each side of their necks, the white bits just touching together at the back but not at the front.

So now we've painted them in our minds, I hope you can imagine Mr and Mrs Wood Pigeon sitting on the long curved branch in the old silver birch tree in the garden.

It's spring time, and all day long Mr and Mrs Wood Pigeon have been building a nest among the dark pink flowers of a cherry tree. Mr Wood Pigeon flies backwards and forwards to other trees up the street, finding dead twigs and pulling them off. Every time he gets one he glides back and pokes it in among the others on a fork in the cherry tree. Then Mrs Wood Pigeon sits on it to make sure no one else comes along and steals the twigs. She doesn't want Mr Wood Pigeon's hard work to be wasted.

They've been doing that nearly all day. But now it's time for a rest. That's why they are sitting on the long curved branch in the old silver birch tree. They have been sitting there ever such a long time. I wonder if you can guess what they are doing?

You know what it's like when you get an itch in the middle of your back, just in that place where you can't reach it? Well, birds have got a place like that. Only in their case it's where their beaks can't reach — round their necks and the back of their heads.

So Mr and Mrs Wood Pigeon are giving each other a good old scratch round their necks. They peck and preen each other and make the smart white collars look even smarter. Sometimes it's Mr Wood Pigeon's turn to do it for Mrs Wood Pigeon. Sometimes it's Mrs Wood Pigeon's turn to do it for Mr Wood Pigeon. And sometimes they both do it to each other at the same time. Sometimes it even looks as though they are whispering secrets in each others' ears! Perhaps they are.

I think Mr and Mrs Wood Pigeon must be very much in love. I think it must be nice to be building your nest together and looking forward to laying eggs and raising a family of baby Wood Pigeons. When they come along, Mr and Mrs Wood Pigeon will be *very* busy finding food to feed their hungry chicks. They will be up at the crack of dawn, flying backwards and forwards with tasty things to eat and poking them into gaping yellow beaks. Very tiring that will be.

But there's no need to think about that yet, not while it's still spring time. Just for now, it must be very pleasant to sit on a long curved branch in an old silver birch tree with someone you love and preen each others' neck feathers. Don't you think so?

- Sing the song.

BIBLE BACKGROUND

Blossoms appear through all the land.
The time has come to sing.
The cooing of doves is heard in our land
Song of Solomon 2:12

LIFE IS A BEAUTIFUL THING

T (P) C

LITTLE BOY SICK

A well-known story from the historical records of the life of Jesus. Using toys or puppets to accompany the song helps children develop their empathy and imagination.

RESOURCES

- Seven or eight dolls, soft toys, or puppets.

CLASS PREPARATION (Optional)

- Children could make stick puppets of the characters in the story.

ASSEMBLY

- Talk about being poorly. Who has been ill and had to stay in bed? Who has had a doctor come to see them? Who has been in hospital?
- **A story: The boy who got better right on time**

  A long time ago, when Jesus lived in Galilee, there were no hospitals, no chemists' shops, and very few medicines. So when little Simeon stopped running around with the other children and said he didn't feel well, his mother began to get worried. She made him some porridge from barley and goat's milk, but Simeon didn't feel like eating anything. He just wanted to lie on his bed shivering, even though the air was as hot as the hottest summer's day in England. There weren't any thermometers in those days, but his mum felt his hot forehead and knew he had a fever. She sat beside him, stroking his head and wiping the sweat from his face with a damp cloth.

  Simeon's dad had an important job. He was one of the king's officers. He was very good at getting things done, but there was nothing he could do to make little Simeon better. He watched him getting weaker and weaker each day.

  Simeon's family lived in the same town as Jesus, so they had heard lots about him. Simeon's dad hadn't been very interested in listening to Jesus. He had been far too busy with his work for the king. But now he remembered how people in the town said that Jesus had made a lot of sick people better. The trouble was, Jesus had gone on a journey to another part of the country. No one knew when he was coming back home again.

Then late one afternoon someone arrived in the town with news that Jesus *had* come back to Galilee, only he was staying in a village twenty miles away, a place called Cana. Simeon's dad set off at once. For the first few miles he travelled along the road he knew so well, the road to the king's palace. The beautiful Sea of Galilee was close by, but he was far too worried to care about the view. After a few miles he stopped for the night at a friend's house. The next morning he turned off the road to the palace and finally arrived at Cana just after midday. It didn't take him long to find out where Jesus was.

'Please, sir,' said Simeon's dad to Jesus, 'please come back home with me and make my son better.'

Jesus looked at the king's officer and shook his head sadly. 'You weren't very interested in listening to me before, were you? But now you need a miracle you come running to get me.'

'Please,' said Simeon's dad, 'if you don't come now my little boy is going to die. Nothing can save him.'

Jesus smiled at him. 'Go on home,' he said. 'Your son is going to live.'

Simeon's dad looked at Jesus. Suddenly he felt sure that what Jesus said was true. He set off at once on the long walk back home.

He spent the night at the house of a friend once more, and then set off again early next morning. He hadn't gone far when he saw some of the men who worked for him running to meet him.

'Your wife sent us,' they panted. 'He's well! Simeon's better! He's sitting up and eating.'

'That's wonderful,' said Simeon's dad. 'What time did he start to get better?'

'The fever left him at about one o'clock yesterday afternoon,' said the men.

'One o'clock!' said Simeon's dad. 'That's exactly the time that Jesus told me that my son was going to live. Jesus did it! He really did it. From now on I'm going to listen to what Jesus says. And so are all my family.'

- Teach the song: Little Boy Sick.
- Choose seven or eight children to hold the dolls, toys or puppets. One toy represents Jesus, another is Simeon, others are his mum and dad and some of the people who listen to Jesus. The children are going to make the toys do actions to fit the song. Talk through suggestions for actions for each line of the song, then try it out.

Choose another group of children and repeat the song.

BIBLE BACKGROUND

The story is found in John 4:43–54.

The officer said, 'Sir, come before my child dies.' Jesus answered, 'Go. Your son will live.'

John 4:49–50

LITTLE BOY SICK

NOD YOUR HEAD IF YOU'VE GOT A BED

Thinking about some of the many things we have to be thankful for. The song requires actions, and may not be suitable for a whole school assembly.

RESOURCES

- A clock face with movable hands.
- Possibly a story and picture of a needy person in the Third World, as found in aid agencies' literature, eg Oxfam, TEAR Fund, Christian Aid.

ASSEMBLY

- Set the clock to 7 o'clock. Ask the children what time it shows. What are they usually doing at 7 o'clock in the morning? Most will still be in bed. Let's say 'thank you' for nice, warm beds.

  Work through the day similarly. Suggestions:

  - 8 o'clock — thank you for breakfast to eat
  - 9 o'clock — thank you for our lovely school
  - 10.30 — thank you for games to play
  - 11 o'clock — thank you for songs to sing
  - 12 o'clock — thank you for food to give us energy
  - 1 o'clock — thank you for stories to read
  - 3.30 — thank you for mums to collect us at the gate
  - 5 o'clock — thank you for TV programmes to watch
  - 7 o'clock — thank you for water to wash in and brush our teeth
  - 7.30 — thank you for bedtime stories and cuddles.

- We have a song about things to be thankful for. Some of them are things we have already thought of. Some of them are funny. Some of them are things we take for granted, like the clean water that comes out of our taps.

  Teach the song.

- The contrast could be made with a Third World situation, where food may be in short supply and no clean water is available at all. All through the day we have things to be thankful for.

BIBLE BACKGROUND

You are praised from where the sun rises to where it sets.

David in Psalm 65:8

NOD YOUR HEAD

C

READY, STEADY

Another of the classic stories that all children should be familiar with. The emphasis is on where we go to find help when we need it.

RESOURCES

- None needed.

ASSEMBLY

◆ We all need people to help us every day. Often it is something very simple, like asking an assistant in a shop where to find something. Sometimes there are more serious things, like if you have an accident.

Who can tell us where to get help when these things happen?

- If you want to know how to spell a word? Look in your spellings book or ask the teacher.
- If there is an accident or a fire? Phone 999 or press the fire alarm.
- If you want to know what's on TV? Look in a magazine.
- If you've got toothache? Go to a dentist.
- If your hair is too long? Go to a hairdresser's or a barber's.
- If you are hungry? Look in the fridge or go to a shop.
- If you have tummy-ache? Go to the doctor.
- If you are frightened? Talk to a grown-up or ring Childline.
- etc.

We are very lucky today because there are lots of places we can go to get help and lots of people ready to help us. Here is a story about a person who had good friends to help him, but he needed help from someone else, too.

◆ **A story: The man who walked home**

Some people can't walk, perhaps because they have had an accident, or because an illness has paralysed their legs. 'Paralysed' means not being able to move part of your body. People who can't walk often have a wheelchair so that they can get around. Some people get very good at moving their wheelchair around fast. They play sports, like basketball.

In the time of Jesus, there weren't any wheelchairs. People who couldn't walk had to stay at home unless someone carried them where they wanted to go. There is a story in the Bible about someone like this. He was paralysed. We don't know what his name was, but we'll call him Daniel. Fortunately, Daniel had some very good friends, friends who didn't mind carrying him places.

One day, Jesus was at home. His home at that time was his friend Peter's house. Peter was a fisherman, and he lived in a town called Capernaum, right next to the beautiful sea of Galilee.

Capernaum was crowded that day. Its narrow streets were packed with people who had come from miles around. Some important people had even come from as far as Jerusalem. They hadn't come because it was the seaside and they wanted a day out, they had come to listen to Jesus and find out about him.

Daniel's friends had heard about Jesus, too. They had heard stories about Jesus making sick people better. If there was any chance that he could do something for Daniel, they wanted to be sure he got that chance. They had set out early that morning, carrying Daniel on a mat, one at each corner. Even for four strong young men it was hard work!

By the time they got to Capernaum they were hot and tired. They didn't need to ask where Jesus' house was, they could see the crowds all gathered round. There were so many people, it was impossible to get anywhere near. How were they going to get Daniel to see Jesus?

The four friends did a bit of hard thinking. They had used their muscles to get this far, now they needed to use their brains. They sat in the shade of a palm tree on the beach getting their breath back. Nearby were some fishing boats and piles of fishing nets and ropes and.... Ropes! That was it! One of the young men had a brainwave.

They picked up Daniel on his mat, borrowed a couple of ropes, and found their way to the side of the house where Jesus was. There was a stone staircase leading up to the flat roof of the house. People in those days used their roofs like an extra room. It was hot work getting Daniel up the steep steps.

Once on the roof, they started pulling up some of the flat tiles. There were shouts from inside, but that didn't stop them. Soon, there was a hole in the roof, a hole big enough to get Daniel through. They tied the ropes around him and lowered him down through the ceiling.

Four faces peered through the hole into the darkness. There was Daniel on the floor, where they had lowered him. All around were important people.

They had been showered in dirt and spiders from the hole in the roof, so they weren't looking very pleased!

A man in the middle looked up at them and gave them a big smile. He didn't seem to mind the dirt and the spiders. That must be Jesus. Then he looked down at Daniel and started talking to him. The friends couldn't quite hear what Jesus was saying, but some of the faces of the important people looked even more cross than before.

Then Jesus spoke to Daniel again, and something amazing happened. Daniel stood up! His legs were working! He wasn't paralysed any more. He picked up his mat, pushed his way through the crowd, and walked out into the street.

The four friends almost fell down the steps in their excitement. Everyone in the street was pushing to see, and slapping Daniel on the back, and praising God. 'We've never seen anything like this!' they said.

That evening, as the sun was setting over the sea of Galilee, five young men in high spirits made their way along the road back to their own village. Just a few hours earlier, one of them had been carried down that road on a mat. Now he was walking home. He had his four friends and Jesus to thank for that.

◆ There are lots of people and places we can go to for help. And often, we can help others, like the four friends who helped Daniel in the story. Daniel didn't have a wheelchair. He couldn't have got to see Jesus on his own. He needed some strong friends to help him.

And when we have nowhere else to go for help, the Bible says we can ask Jesus to help us. Here is a song that says that. It is called, 'Ready, Steady, Go!' Maybe Daniel and his friends were saying 'Ready, steady, go!' and having races on their way home.

◆ Teach the song.

BIBLE BACKGROUND

The story is found in Mark 2:1–12.

The people were amazed and praised God.
They said, 'We have never seen anything like this!'
Mark 2:12

READY, STEADY, GO TO JESUS

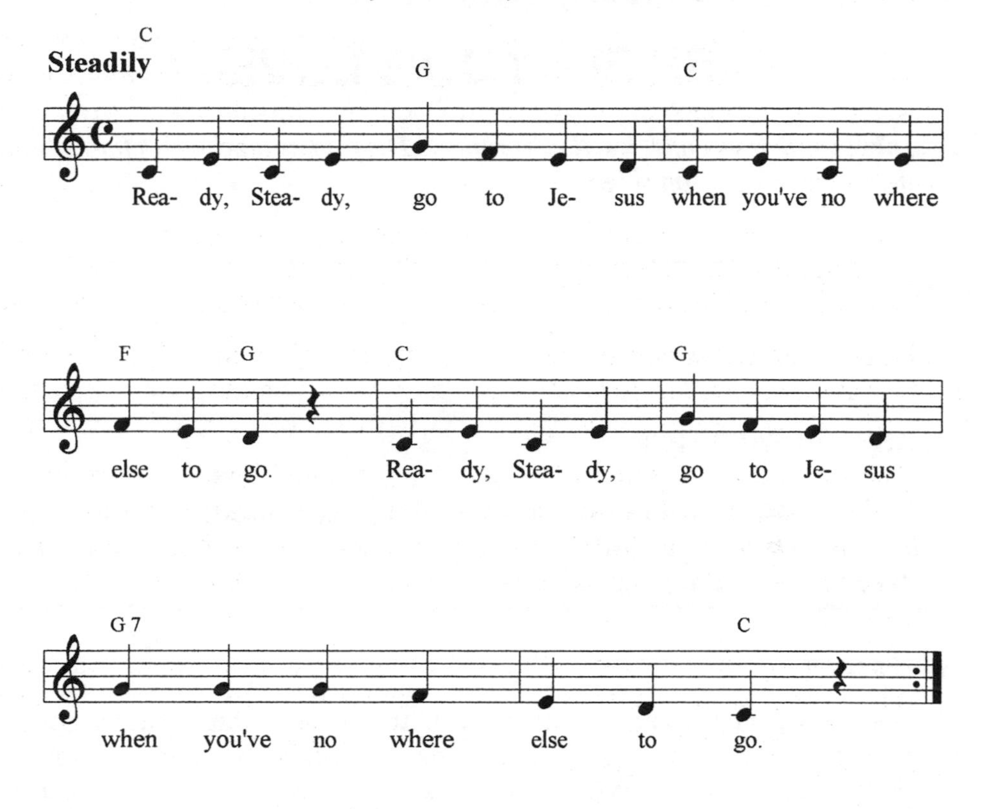

If space allows children can get into a starting position like an athlete and on the word 'go' spring forward and continue running on the spot.

SHOW YOUR LOVE

Learning to show our appreciation of others. The song is a good one for selecting the mood you want to finish on.

RESOURCES

- Art and craft materials.

CLASS PREPARATION

- With the class, draw up a list of people we appreciate because of who they are or what they do for us. Talk about practical ways to show our appreciation. Make cards, pictures, etc., as below.

ASSEMBLY

◆ Loving people means appreciating them, and showing them that we appreciate them. There are lots of ways of doing this. You show your gran you love her by giving her a hug. When someone sings a song, or reads a poem or presents a play, we show we appreciate them by giving them a clap.

Here is a song all about different ways of showing our love and appreciation to people.

Teach the song.

◆ There are lots more ways of showing people we appreciate them. *Class 3* is going to show us some of the things they have made for people they appreciate.

The children show and talk about their items. Where possible, they can actually be presented to their intended recipients. Suggestions:

- a thank-you letter for the dinner ladies
- a model for the caretaker
- a posy of flowers for the secretary
- stickers for the cleaners
- a promise to help with the dishes for mum

- a 'welcome to our school' card for a visitor
- a 'get well' card for someone who is poorly
- a friendship bracelet for the crossing person.

All these are practical ways of showing people we love and appreciate them. One of Jesus' disciples was called John. John wrote a letter to people all about love. It is part of the Bible. John said that our love should not only be words and talk. We should show our love by what we do.

Perhaps other people would like to follow the example of *Class 3* and think of ways to show how they appreciate people.

◆ End with the song again. Depending on what words you use for the last verse, this is good for quietening a group down, or finishing on whatever mood you want.

BIBLE BACKGROUND

My children, our love should not only be in words and talk. Our love must be true love. And we should show that love by what we do.

The Apostle John in 1 John 3:18

SHOW YOUR LOVE

2. **Show your love with a hug, hug, hug.** ***(give yourself a hug)***
3. **Show your love with a wave, wave, wave.** ***(wave)***
4. **Show your love with a kiss, kiss, kiss.** ***(make kissing sound with lips)***
5. **Show your love with a jump, jump, jump.** ***(jump)***
6. **Show your love with a shh, shh, shh.** ***(put one finger to lips)***

Repeat verse one (as a bit of a surprise) if appropriate.

S

THANK YOU, GOD, FOR EYES THAT SEE

Learning about light and colour. This assembly can be used as a Harvest talk.

RESOURCES

- Fruit and vegetables of as many different colours as possible, including black (grapes, aubergine) and white; a picture or drawing of a rainbow; a table. Alternatively, use flowers instead of fruit and vegetables.

ASSEMBLY

- Show the children the fruit and vegetables one at a time, saying what they are, and ask what colour each one is. They will find some of the colours easy, and need help naming others.

  Ask some of the children which are their favourite colours, or which fruit they think looks the nicest.

  Now a hard question: What makes the fruit and vegetables different colours? The answer is: light.

  Light is made of all the colours of the rainbow. (Show a picture of a rainbow.) Sometimes people say that there are seven colours in a rainbow. Who knows what they are? Red, orange, yellow, green, blue, indigo and violet. Really, there are millions of colours, each a tiny bit different from the next. But if we are painting a rainbow, it is easier just to paint seven colours.

  Get a volunteer to come and help lay the fruit and vegetables out on the table in rainbow order. White and black ones get left out for the moment.

  Let's go back to our hard question: What makes the fruit and vegetables different colours? The answer was... ? Light.

  Light hits a tomato, and the tomato skin bounces back just the red part of the rainbow. So we see a red tomato.

  Light hits a banana, and the banana skin bounces back just the yellow part of the rainbow. So we see a yellow banana.

  Light hits a lettuce, and the lettuce leaves bounce back just the green part of the rainbow. So we see a green lettuce.

Isn't that clever!

What about white leeks and black grapes? When light hits the white part of a leek, the leek bounces back all the colours of the rainbow. And all the colours of the rainbow together make white.

Black grapes are just the opposite. The skin of the grape doesn't bounce any of the colours of the rainbow back at all. So the grapes look black.

This isn't just clever, it is also very useful. Who likes eating nice ripe, red tomatoes? Lots of people. And who likes eating unripe, green tomatoes? No one. We can see at once if a tomato, or a strawberry, or a cherry is ripe and ready to eat. It turns red. If we couldn't see the difference between red tomatoes and green tomatoes, we would have to keep taking bites and spitting out the green bits until we found a ripe one. Yuk!

So here are two wonderful things: fruit and vegetables in all the colours of the rainbow, and eyes to see them.

Does anyone know what the Bible says was the very first thing God created at the beginning of the world? It is something we have been talking about. (Not tomatoes!) Light.

On the very first page of the Bible it says this: **'God said, "Let there be light!" And there was light. God saw that the light was good.'**

Everyone can agree with God: light is good. It is good because it is useful. It is good because it makes the world interesting and beautiful to look at.

Let's say 'thank you' to God for making so many different fruit and vegetables, and for the light that gives them all the colours of the rainbow, and for eyes to see them.

- Teach the song. The children might be asked to suggest different verses of their own. This song works well accompanied by sign language. Perhaps you have someone who can teach the children the appropriate signs.

BIBLE BACKGROUND

The Lord God made all kinds of trees grow out of the ground — trees that were pleasing to the eye and good for food.

Genesis 2:9

THANK YOU GOD

THANK YOU, GOD, YOU'RE FANTASTIC

Naming jobs and countries helps us learn about the inclusiveness of God's love.

RESOURCES

- A length of elastic, 2½ to 3 metres, tied in a circle; a globe.

ASSEMBLY

- Show the circle of elastic. This circle is like God's love. God's love stretches and stretches and stretches. God wants all sorts of people inside his circle of love.

  Let's think of all the different kinds of job people do. It might be something your mum or your dad does, or an aunty, or a granddad. Hands up who can tell me a job someone does?

  As children name different jobs, bring them out and stand them inside the circle of elastic. Continue until there are eight to ten children in the circle.

  We could go on thinking of lots and lots more jobs. God loves all the people who do those jobs, and all the others we could think of, and all the people who haven't got a job. God's circle of love is stretchier than our circle of elastic. God's love goes on stretching for ever and ever.

  Send those children back to their places.

  Now let's see how many children we have here who have come from different countries, or whose parents came from different countries, or who have relatives or friends in different countries. Can you tell us the names of those countries?

  As children name different countries, bring them out to stand in the circle as before. If you are somewhere where there are few children to whom this applies (or perhaps it will make the ones to whom it does not apply stand out), ask the children to name different countries that they know of.

  When the circle is fairly full, show the globe.

  There are lots more countries in the world which we have never even heard of. God loves all the people in those countries, too. Let's get someone in the circle to hold the globe. Now think how big God's circle of love is. It's not just big enough to hold these people here, it stretches right round the world! Just think how big a piece of elastic we should need to go all the way round the world!

It says in the Bible that God's love is bigger than any person can ever know. It is so big, nobody is outside it. Wherever you go, whatever you do, you will never be outside the circle of God's love.

- Send the children back to their places and teach the song. It could be sung several times, with a different child holding up the globe each time to remind everybody how big God's love is.

BIBLE BACKGROUND

Christ's love is greater than any person can ever know.
But I pray that you will be able to know that love.
The Apostle Paul in Ephesians 3:19

THANK YOU GOD YOU'RE FANTASTIC

To the tune of
What Shall We do With the Drunken Sailor? **Traditional**

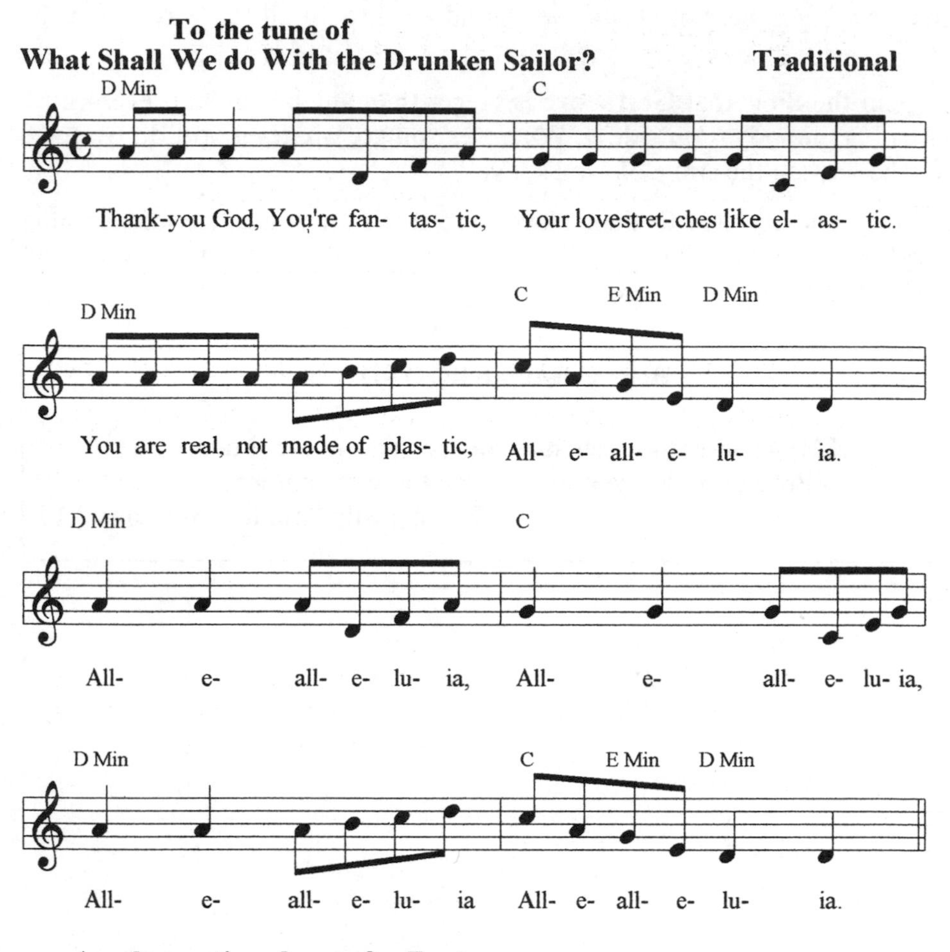

An alternative chorus for Easter:

Hooray and up He rises
Hooray and up He rises
Hooray and up He rises
Early in the morning.

C

THERE'S MORE THAN ME IN MY FAMILY

Families are important, and they come in all sorts of shapes and sizes.

RESOURCES

- A picture board; pictures of families of animals with babies; a human family.
- These names written on pieces of paper: Israel; Leah, Rachel, Bilhah and Zilpah; Simeon, Judah, Dinah, Joseph and Benjamin.

ASSEMBLY

◆ Show the animal pictures and talk about them.

Bring out the fact that there are all sorts of animal families. Sometimes there is one male and several females (as in a family of lions). Sometimes one male and one female stay together for life (as in several species of birds). Sometimes babies are born and have to survive on their own straight away (like baby turtles and most fish). Sometimes the parents look after their babies for a few months (like birds or rabbits). A few animals look after their young for several years (elephants do).

The animals that look after their young the longest are people. Human children need caring for until they are teenagers. That is why families are very important.

Human families are very different, too.

◆ There is a very famous family in the Bible. There was one dad in this family. He had two names. When he was young, his name was Jacob. Later on, when he had grown up and had children, God gave him a new name: Israel. (Show name.)

There were four mums in this family. Their names were Leah, Rachel, Bilhah and Zilpah.

As you can imagine, there were lots of children in this family. Here are the names of some of them: Simeon, Judah, Dinah, Joseph and Benjamin. Is there anyone here who has the same name as one of the children in this family?

When these children grew up, they had families of their own. Just think how many cousins there must have been! Each of these families became a whole tribe of people. They all called themselves 'the children of Israel'. Later on, the country God gave them to live in was also called Israel.

A long, long time after that, Jesus was born into one of those families, the family that went all the way back to Judah.

- Who would like to tell us about their own family?

Get one or two children to talk about the names and relationships in their family.

- The Bible tells us lots of stories about Israel's family. It also tells us about a different sort of family, a family that *anyone* can belong to. It says that Jesus came to show people that anyone can belong to God's family. Jesus called God his Father. He came to show that we can know God as our Father, too, and be God's children.

That is why the prayer that Jesus taught us begins, 'Our Father in heaven.... '

So, although everybody's family is different, anyone who wants to can be part of God's family, the biggest family on earth. Nobody need feel left out.

- Teach the song.

BIBLE BACKGROUND

But some people did accept him. They believed in him. To them he gave the right to become children of God.

The Apostle John, writing about Jesus in John 1:12

THERE'S MORE THAN ME IN MY FAMILY

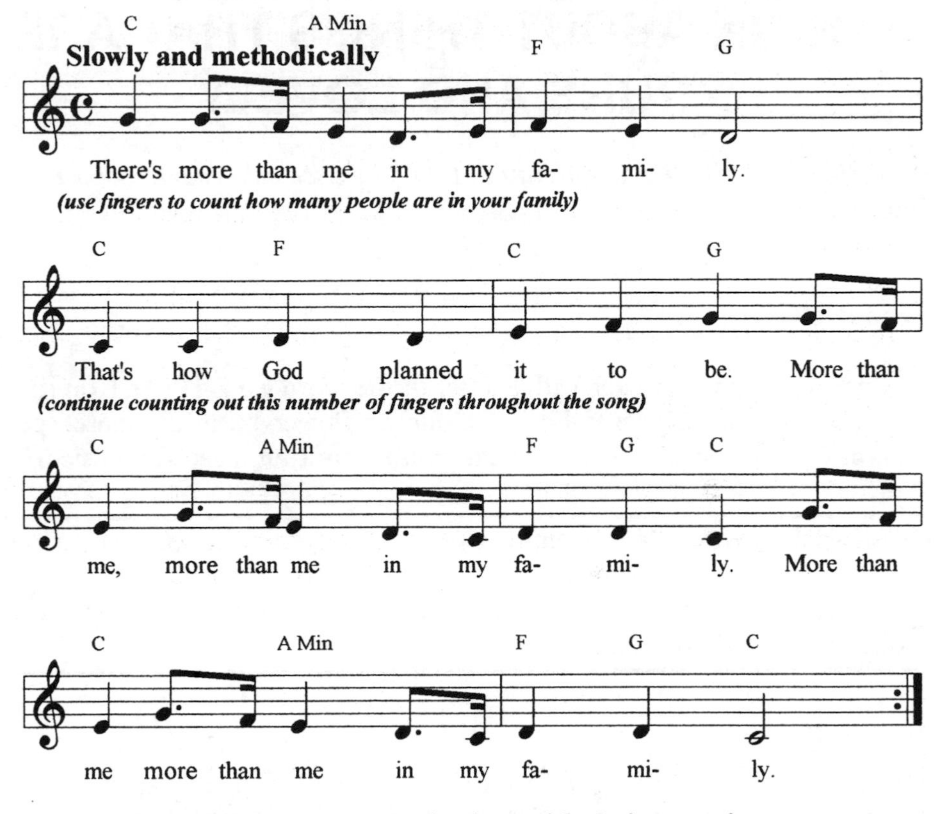

See if the children can keep in time with their counting.
If children find it difficult to remember how many to count, let them just count all their fingers in turn.

(P) C

THINK ABOUT THINGS THAT ARE PURE AND LOVELY

Reflecting on things that are beautiful. Could be used as a counterpoint to Hallowe'en.

RESOURCES

- Nine sheets of paper each with a letter of the word **b e a u t i f u l** on it; a picture of something beautiful on each one, eg flower, butterfly, sunset, person, painting, etc.; perhaps some flowers; some beautiful, peaceful music to play.

CLASS PREPARATION (Optional)

- Children could prepare the sheets as above, finding suitable pictures to cut out and stick on the sheets.

ASSEMBLY

◆ Bring out children one at a time to hold up the sheets of paper. Talk about each picture. Why is it beautiful? The colours, shape, smile.

When all nine are in a line, hold up the sheets and ask the children what word the letters make: **beautiful**. The Bible tells people to think about things that are beautiful, and pure, and lovely. When we look at beautiful things, it makes us feel good inside. It makes us feel peaceful.

Now move the children holding the letters **l i f e** to one side. Ask the children what word these letters make.

Look at all the pictures again. Which ones are things that are *alive*? (Eg birds, animals, plants, people.) Which ones are not alive? (Eg sunset, crystals.)

Even the ones that are not alive need someone alive to appreciate them. If there was no one to see the sunset, no one would know it was beautiful.

Look at the letters which are left: **b a u t u** . What do they spell? Nothing! On their own they don't mean anything. We need to put **l i f e** back again. (Move the children to restore **beautiful**.)

Ask the children to quietly choose the picture they like best and imagine it inside their head. Remember that the Bible tells people to think about things that are beautiful, and pure, and lovely.

Have a moment of quiet. It could be suggested to children that they pray quietly and say thank you to God for the beautiful thing they are thinking of.

- Teach the song.
- End by listening to some beautiful music and thinking about more beautiful things, perhaps the flowers, or something they want to imagine.

BIBLE BACKGROUND

Think about things that are true and honourable and right and pure and beautiful and respected.

The Apostle Paul in Philippians 4:8

THINK ABOUT THINGS THAT ARE PURE AND LOVELY

THINK ABOUT WHAT YOU CAN GIVE

Visual aids help children to understand some of Jesus' teaching about the fruits of generosity.

RESOURCES

- Two boxes, one with **mine** written on the front, the other with **give away** on the front and **Jesus** on the back, the latter written on yellow or gold paper if possible.
- Some small sweets; some coins, eg £1 in silver; some small toys; two pieces of paper with clock faces drawn on them, one larger than the other.

ASSEMBLY

- Show the sweets. Ask the children to imagine that they have been given these sweets. Either use one volunteer or ask the children generally, how many would they keep to eat themselves and how many would they share with other people? Show the two boxes with the words **mine** and **give away**. Everyone has an invisible **mine** box and an invisible **give away** box. Put sweets in the boxes according to the child's or children's response.

  Now do the same with the money. This could be made more concrete by, for example, suggesting that they have been given £1 by their gran. There is a collection in school for (name of a charity the school supports). How much would they keep and how much give away?

  It is not only money we can give to help other people; we can give time, too. Show clock faces. One way of giving time to help other people is to do a sponsored spell or sponsored swim. Other ways are spending time helping mum at home, or spending time being friendly with someone who is lonely. Ask the children if they are willing to give away some of their time. According to their responses, put clock faces in the two boxes. The larger clock face will probably go in the **mine** box to show that we give away less time than we keep for ourselves.

  Toys can also be used. How much do we keep them for ourselves and how much do we share them and let other people play with them?

  Now talk about growing up. Shall we go on sharing as we grow up? Grown-ups have more money and things than children. In a grown-up's **mine** box there might be a house, and a car, and lots of furniture, and maybe lots of money. How much might there be in a grown-up's **give away** box? How much will there be in our **give away** box when we are grown-ups?

Eventually, we shall all get old and finally die. Hold up the **mine** box. This box is probably quite full by the time someone dies. Can they take this box full of things with them? No. There is a well-known saying, 'You can't take it with you when you die.'

Hold up the **give away** box and turn it round. What does it say on the back? **Jesus.** Jesus told his followers that every time they gave something away, it was the same as giving it to him. Every time they helped someone, it was the same as helping him. So every time we give away our money or our time to help someone, it is the same as giving it to Jesus. The **give away** box is also the **Jesus** box.

Where does Jesus live? In heaven. Jesus gave his followers a promise. He promised them that everything they gave away, he would keep for them in heaven. Then, when a person dies, Jesus promises to give back to them all the things in their **give away** box, only lots more as well!

Jesus said that this was 'storing up treasure in heaven'. The more we share with other people on earth, the more we give away, the more treasure we have stored up and waiting for us in heaven.

◆ Teach the song.

BIBLE BACKGROUND

Anything you did for any of my people here, you also did for me.
Jesus in Matthew 25:40

Get the treasure in heaven that never runs out.
Thieves can't steal it in heaven, and moths can't destroy it.
Jesus in Luke 12:33

THINK ABOUT WHAT YOU CAN GIVE

WE MAKE PEOPLE HAPPY WHEN WE PRAY

An 'instant drama' story helps us to understand a little more about praying.

RESOURCES

- Three tea-towels as token 'Eastern' head-dresses; two PE mats for children to lie on. Draw the curtains or blinds to make the room or hall dim.

ASSEMBLY

- Ask for eight children to help with a story. Manoeuvre them to act out the story as you tell it.
- **A story: The friend at midnight**

  This is a story that Jesus told, so it happened nearly two thousand years ago. Five of the helpers are one family. We shall call them Matthias (with a tea-towel head-dress) and his wife and three children. It is night-time, so they are all asleep in their house. (Get Matthias and his family to lie down on one of the PE mats.)

  Nearby in the same village live Amos (another tea-towel) and his wife. They are friends with Matthias and his family. They have gone to bed, too. (Amos and his wife lie down on the second PE mat.)

  We have one person left. We'll call him Melki (the last tea-towel). Melki isn't asleep. He has been walking all day, and he is very tired and hungry. He is on a long journey, and he hopes to spend the night at Amos' house. (There weren't any telephones in those days, so Melki couldn't phone his old friend Amos to let him know he was coming.)

  At last he finds Amos' house in the dark and knocks on the door. A sleepy Amos and his wife let him in. They are really pleased to see their old friend. They sit him down on the mat and get him a drink. But, oh dear! There is nothing in the house to eat, nothing at all. What are they going to do?

  Ask the children for suggestions. (There are no shops to go to; letting a guest go hungry would be unthinkable. Someone is sure to suggest going to Matthias' house to borrow some food.)

So Amos goes out into the dark alleyway and knocks on his friend's door. Knock, knock! Knock, knock! Inside Matthias groans and rolls over in bed. Knock, knock! goes Amos on the door again.

'Matthias,' he calls, 'It's me, Amos. An old friend has just arrived on a journey. We've got nothing to eat in the house. Please could you lend me three small loaves of bread?'

Matthias groans again. 'Go away,' he says. 'The door is locked. We're all asleep. You are disturbing the children. I can't get up now and give you bread.'

But then his wife nudges him in the ribs. 'You've got to,' she whispers. 'Amos has a guest. If we don't give him something to eat, it will bring shame on the whole village. What will people say? A visitor comes to town and we let him go hungry? It will be a disgrace.'

Matthias groans again. He knows it is true. He won't be able to hold his head up if he lets Amos down. He rubs his eyes, rolls out of bed, and finds some bread for Amos to give the unexpected guest.

Amos goes back home and feeds his friend Melki. At last everybody can settle to sleep. They all know they have done the right thing.

- Thank the helpers and send them back to their places.

In Jesus' time, looking after visitors properly was very important. What Matthias' wife said was quite true. It would be a disgrace to the whole village if a visitor was allowed to go hungry. It is a bit like when a visitor comes to our school. If someone does something silly, it lets the whole school down. Everyone feels bad.

Jesus said that Amos knocking on his friend's door was like us talking to God. When we have a real need we can talk to God in prayer. Only God doesn't go to sleep or get grumpy like Matthias. Matthias gave Amos some bread for his friend because it was the right thing to do. God always does what is right, so God will hear our prayers and do what is right when we ask him.

Jesus wanted to encourage people to pray, to talk to God. When we pray, we can say things like, 'My friend is in trouble, please help her.' Or, 'My friend needs something, please help me to help him.'

So whenever we see someone in trouble, or someone in need, we can be like Amos. We can go knocking on God's invisible door and ask him to help.

- Teach the song.
- Some children could make up their own prayers along the lines suggested.

BIBLE BACKGROUND

The story is found in Luke 11:5–8.

So I tell you, continue to ask, and God will give to you....
Continue to knock, and the door will open for you.

Jesus in Luke 11:9

WE MAKE PEOPLE HAPPY WHEN WE PRAY

It is also helpful to find out the BSL or Maketon signs for these verbs.

Other suggestions for verses are:

We make people happy when we smile
give
care
help
sing
share
clap

WHEN I DRAW A CROSS LIKE THIS

A simple but effective illustration to teach about love. Could be used at Easter or, perhaps, for St Valentine's day.

RESOURCES

- OHP; two blank OHP acetates and pens. (Or paper flip-pad and pens.)

ASSEMBLY

- Draw a traditional Christian cross on the OHP using single lines. Ask the children what it is. Give as much explanation as necessary. We might call it a **Jesus-cross**. When people see a cross like this, it makes them think of Jesus. Some people wear a cross like this on a chain around their necks.

  On a fresh acetate, draw the kind of cross used to represent a kiss on the bottom of a letter. Talk about this kind of cross and how it is used. We might call this one a **kiss-cross**. If you get a birthday card from your gran with a cross on it like this, you know your gran is telling you she loves you.

  Replace the **Jesus-cross**. This cross also tells us that someone loves us. It reminds us that God loves us and Jesus loves us.

  What happens if we put the **kiss-cross** on top of the **Jesus-cross**? What have we got now? A star.

  Who remembers how the Wise Men found the baby Jesus in the Christmas story? They followed a star, a special star that moved in the sky and led them to Bethlehem.

  We do not have that special star in the sky now. But there are still lots and lots of other stars that we can look up at on a dark clear night. Who likes looking at the stars?

  One of the old songs in the Bible talks about how God made the stars and says that they show how God loves us, too. This is what it says:

  He made the moon and stars to rule the night.
  His love continues for ever.

So now we have three things that remind us of how much we are loved: the cross that makes us think of Jesus and how much he loves us (show on the OHP again); the kiss-cross that tells us that our gran or a friend loves us; and the star when I put the two together that reminds us of God who loves us and who made the stars in the sky.

- Teach the song. The children can make the cross and star signs with their fingers in the air as they sing the song.

BIBLE BACKGROUND

He made the moon and stars to rule the night.
His love continues for ever.
Psalm 136:9

Note: One interpretation of the Anthropic Principle (which states that the universe appears to be very finely tuned for the existence of human life) is that it is evidence of the design of a creator God. On this interpretation, modern science may be seen as concurring with the psalmist that the billions of stars in the universe reflect the divine love of the creator.

WHEN I DRAW A CROSS LIKE THIS

WHEN THINGS GET VERY DARK

A deeply important lesson on the enduring power of goodness that gets children's (and adults') complete attention.

RESOURCES

- A 'magic candle' that relights when blown out (available from shops that sell items for parties); matches. Draw the curtains or blinds to make the room or hall dim. *Important: this talk should be well rehearsed.*

ASSEMBLY

- One of the things Jesus said about himself was, 'I am the light of the world.' In some churches today, a candle is lit at the beginning of the service. It reminds people of Jesus and what he said.

  Light the magic candle and hold it up in front of you.

  One of Jesus' friends wrote this about him: 'The light shines in the darkness, and the darkness has never put it out.'

  We all remember the Christmas story, how Jesus came into the world as a baby. The king at that time was King Herod. King Herod was jealous. He was afraid that people might think this baby should be the king instead of him. So after he had talked to the Wise Men, he sent soldiers to Bethlehem to kill all the little boys under two years old. He wanted to kill the baby Jesus.

  Blow the candle out. Watch in silence until it relights. Then say:

  But, 'The light shines in the darkness, and the darkness has never put it out.'

  An angel had told Joseph in a dream that baby Jesus was in danger. So Mary and Joseph and Jesus had escaped to another country, Egypt. They stayed there until it was safe to go home again.

  Jesus grew up. One day he went to talk to the people in the Jewish synagogue in Nazareth. Some of the people there didn't like the things Jesus said. They got so angry, they wanted to kill him. They took him to a cliff to throw him off.

  Blow the candle out, as before.

  But, 'The light shines in the darkness, and the darkness has never put it out.'

  Jesus turned and walked through the crowd of men. They could not stop him.

Another time, Jesus was in a boat on the Sea of Galilee. He was so tired, he fell fast asleep. While he was asleep, a big storm blew up. The wind howled and the waves crashed over the boat. Even the fishermen in the boat were sure they were all going to drown.

Blow the candle out, as before.

But, 'The light shines in the darkness, and the darkness has never put it out.'

Jesus stood up and told the storm to be quiet. The wind and the waves calmed down, and everyone was safe.

Finally, the chief priests in Jerusalem arrested Jesus. They beat him and put a cruel crown of thorns on his head. Then they nailed him to a wooden cross and left him to die.

Blow out the candle.

This time, Jesus really was dead. They took his body and laid it in a tomb, a cave in the rock. Then they rolled a big stone over the entrance. (If the candle relights as you are saying this, simply keep blowing it out.)

Watch in silence until the candle relights.

But, 'The light shines in the darkness, and the darkness has never put it out.'

On Easter Sunday morning, Jesus' friends came to the tomb. It was empty, and the stone was rolled away.

Then one of the friends, Mary, saw Jesus. He was alive. He spoke to her.

That evening he came to the room where all his friends were gathered. Later he promised to be with them, even to the end of the world.

All down through the years, bad people have tried to put out the light. Sometimes good people have been killed.

But, 'The light shines in the darkness, and the darkness has never put it out.'

The light still shines today, and it goes on growing brighter all over the world.

- Teach the song.

BIBLE BACKGROUND

The light shines in the darkness, and the darkness has never put it out.
John 1:5 (*Good News Bible*)

Note: I first saw Peter Green, then of Open Air Campaigners, demonstrate this at a British Youth for Christ training session. It fits so perfectly with Elaine's song, and is such a powerfully effective talk, that I felt it had to be reproduced here. Used by permission.

WHEN THINGS GET VERY DARK

WHERE DO WE FIND JESUS?

Signs from the everyday world and signs from the Bible.

RESOURCES

- A number of easily identifiable signs (see suggestions below). These might be collected, or drawn, or printed from a computer clip-art collection. (Eg the popular Masterclips collections have many suitable signs in the *symbols* directory.) A Bible.

ASSEMBLY

- Show signs one at a time and ask the children if they know what the signs stand for. Give explanations as necessary. Suitable signs could include those for: Post Office, Telephone, Picnic Site, Motorway, Danger, red flag at the beach, Beware of the Dog, No Smoking, Green Man (on pedestrian crossing), Ladies and Gents toilets, Private, etc.
- There are three sorts of signs here. The first sort of sign is a helpful sign. It gives us useful information, like telling us where to find something. A Picnic Site sign is a helpful sign. The second sort of sign is a warning sign. It tells us when or where there might be danger, like the red flag at the beach. The third sort of sign tells us about things that are not allowed. When you see a Private sign on a door you know you are not allowed to go in without permission.

  Three children might be chosen to stand up at the front and hold examples of the three sorts of signs. The rest of the signs could then be looked at again and children asked which group they belong to. Some signs could belong to more than one group.
- Show the Bible. The Bible has lots of signs in it. Sometimes they were things people could see, like a pile of rocks where something important had happened. Sometimes the signs were things God did, like miracles.
- Some of the signs in the Bible are helpful signs, showing people where to look for things that are important. Some of the signs in the Bible are warning signs, telling people about things that are dangerous. There are also signs about things that are not allowed.

Choose one or more of the following stories, either to remind the children if they already know it, or to tell them in more detail. Three of these stories are about helpful signs, and the fourth about warning signs.

- **The story of Noah and the flood, as told in Genesis 6 – 8**

What was the sign God put in the sky? A rainbow. God said to Noah, 'I am putting my rainbow in the clouds. It is a sign of the agreement between me and the earth... Flood waters will never again destroy all life on the earth' (Genesis 9:13,15b). So the rainbow is a helpful sign. It is a reminder of the agreement God made with all the living things on the earth to look after them.

- **The story of the birth of Jesus and the shepherds, as told in Luke 2:1–20**

What was the sign the angel gave to the shepherds so that they could find the infant Saviour? They had to look for 'a baby wrapped in cloths and lying in a manger' (Luke 2:12). That was a helpful sign. For hundreds of years the Jewish people had been expecting a very special person to come, the Saviour, the Messiah. The angel gave the shepherds a sign so that they could go and find him.

- **The story of the LITTLE BOY SICK, John 4:43–54**

(See song and story on pages 129–132.) One of Jesus' followers called John wrote down that story. At the end of the story John said that it was a 'miraculous sign'. The little boy's father had not been very interested in Jesus at first. When the boy was made better, it was a sign that Jesus really was someone very special and very important. After that sign, the father and his whole family believed in Jesus.

- **The story of Moses, Pharaoh, and the ten plagues, as told in Exodus 7 to 11**

The plagues were warning signs to Pharaoh. They showed God's power and how foolish it is to try to stand against God.

- Teach the song.

This song has proved good for using as a beautiful dance.

BIBLE BACKGROUND

Jesus from Nazareth was a very special man. God clearly showed this to you by the miracles, wonders, and signs God did through him.

Peter on the day of Pentecost, Acts 2:22

The LORD showed us great and terrible signs and miracles. He did them to Egypt, the king and his whole family.

Deuteronomy 6:22

WHERE DO WE FIND JESUS?

2nd verse:

Talk to Him always. *(use fingers to move as if speaking)*
He hears you when you cry. *(bow head or hold head in hands)*
That prayer which smells like sweet perfume *(roll hands upwards into the air)*
Makes Jesus feel close by. *(bring arms down into a hug)*

If space allows use the dance movements in italics.

C

WHO GIVES US SNOW IN THE WINTER?

Appreciating how much God does, and an opportunity to say 'thank you'.

RESOURCES

- Ten or so sheets of paper with large 'smiley' faces on them.

ASSEMBLY

◆ The day has only just begun, but already lots of people have been helping us to make it a good day. Let's see how many we can think of.

Who enjoyed having cereal for breakfast? Now think, who grew the corn to make the cereal? A farmer. Let's have one person who enjoyed breakfast cereal to hold a smiley face. Then we can all say, 'Thank you, my friend the farmer.'

Repeat with the following, or similar, as appropriate:

- Who drove the corn to the factory? A lorry-driver.
- Who went shopping and bought the cereal and the milk? Mum.
- Did anyone come to school by bus? Who drove you here? A bus-driver.
- Who helped us cross the road safely? The crossing-lady.
- Who swept the classroom floor last night and cleaned up ready? The cleaner.
- Who unlocked the doors (and put the heating on)? The caretaker.
- Who is working hard in the kitchen to get lunch ready? The dinner ladies.
- Who is coming to school to help us today? (Parent to listen to readers, etc.)

There are so many people who have already helped to make it a good day today, and we could think of lots more if we tried. What a lot of people helping us to have smiley faces!

◆ We've got a song that asks lots of 'Who?' questions like those. Listen to the words of the first verse and see who can tell us the answer to these questions:

Who gives us snow in winter?
Who makes it rain or shine?
Who gives us eyes, two ears and a nose?
Who loves us all the time?

The answer is... God. God who made the earth just the way it is, and all the people in it. Let's have someone hold up a smiley face. Then we can say: 'Thank you, God, for making the earth. Thank you, God, for making me. Thank you, God, for making it a good day.'

- Teach the song.

BIBLE BACKGROUND

God takes care of us richly. He gives us everything to enjoy.
1 Timothy 4:17

WHO GIVES US SNOW IN THE WINTER?

C

WHO IS THE BABY IN THE HAY?

A Christmas message about patience, remembering, and God's promises.

RESOURCES

- A manger; a child-sized shepherd's costume.

ASSEMBLY

- Talk about the excitement of Christmas coming. Ask the children what they are looking forward to most. Ask them if they find it difficult to be patient. When decorations go up so early in the shops, it always seems such a long time to wait.

- If that seems a long time, it was nothing like the first Christmas.

  Choose a volunteer to be one of the shepherds in the Christmas story. Dress him up. Let's say his name is Jacob.

  We need lots of other people to help us with this story, a whole line of people.

  Get a line of eight to ten children standing, with 'Jacob' at one end. Introduce them: the one next to Jacob is his mum (or dad). The next person is his grandad. The next one is his great-grandad. Then his great-great-grandma. Carry on this way to the last but one of the line.

  Actually, to do this properly, we should have a whole class of people in the line — more than thirty. Only if we do that we shall lose count of all the 'great-greats'.

  The last person is someone whose name we do know. It is an unusual name. He is called Micah. Micah lived more than seven hundred years before Jacob. Seven hundred years is an awful lot of great-great grandmas and great-great grandads!

  Micah had a very important job to do. He was a prophet. He spent a lot of time talking to God and listening to God. Then he told the people what God wanted them to hear.

  One day he had an important message from God. This was the message: 'Someone very special is coming. He is going to be born in Bethlehem.'

Let's see if our Micah can remember the message and tell everyone. (Repeat the message and encourage the child to speak it out.)

People got excited. 'When is it going to happen?' they said. 'Will it be soon?' They waited and waited, but nothing happened. If that was us waiting, we should probably have got fed up and forgotten all about it. But those people knew that when God says something, he never lets you down.

So Jacob's great-great-great-great-great-great-great-great-great-grandad passed the message on to his children.

Get the next child in the line to say the message: 'Someone very special is coming. He is going to be born in Bethlehem.' Do this all the way down the line.

So finally, Jacob's mum told Jacob the message. And as he grew up, he stored it away in the back of his mind.

I expect you know the next bit of the story. One day Jacob and some of his friends were taking a flock of sheep to the temple in Jerusalem. They spent the night in fields near Bethlehem, a day's walk from the city.

That night something wonderful happened. An angel appeared and told them that Micah's message was coming true that very night! There was a very special baby born in Bethlehem. It was Jesus, the Saviour.

Jacob and his friends hurried into the village. They found the baby lying in a manger, just like the angel had told them. (Put the manger in front of Jacob, or lead him to it.) Jacob looked at the baby and remembered the message that had come all down the line from his great-great-great-grandparents hundreds of years before. He felt very privileged to be the one who saw it come true.

So, when we feel impatient because Christmas seems like a long time coming, let's remember the people who waited for hundreds and hundreds of years. And let's remember that when God tells people something is going to happen, he always keeps his word.

- Teach the song.

BIBLE BACKGROUND

But you, Bethlehem Ephrathah, are one of the smallest towns in Judah.
But from you will come one who will rule Israel for me.
He comes from very old times, from days long ago.

Micah 5:2

Note: Micah lived in the eighth century before Christ. This prophecy was the one that enabled King Herod's advisers to tell him where the Messiah would be born when the Magi came. See Matthew 2:1–8.

WHO IS THE BABY IN THE HAY?

C

YOU'LL GET BURNT IF YOU PLAY WITH FIRE

A fun lesson in verse on taking care to avoid dangers.

RESOURCES

- None needed.

ASSEMBLY

- This is a story about a cat called Mullarkey. Mullarkey was a tabby cat, that's to say a cat with stripes like a tiger. If you ever met Mullarkey, you would know at once that he was the kind of cat that was always getting into trouble. He had one torn ear, scars on his nose, and his tail had a bend in the middle that would never straighten out.

  People say that cats have nine lives. Mullarkey had got in so many scrapes that he had lost nearly all of his nine lives. This is his story. When I get to the end of each verse, you have to tell me how many lives he had left.

1. Mullarkey didn't stop to look when crossing o'er the street,
   Too late he saw the car race up that knocked him off his feet.
   Mullarkey's tail was squashed quite flat, he looked a sorry state.
   This morning he had nine lives left, but now it's only... (Children fill in: *eight*.)

2. Mullarkey bit the TV wire and pulled it from its socket,
   It went off BANG! and shocked him so he shot off like a rocket.
   Mullarkey thought he must have died and gone to moggy heaven.
   This morning he had eight lives left, but now it's only...

3. Mullarkey tried to steal a fish from out the pond next door,
   The owner caught him in the act and gave a mighty roar.
   Mullarkey streaked off down the path and dodged the flying sticks.
   This morning he had seven lives left, but now it's only...

4. Mullarkey thought it fun to tease the dog next door called Rover,
   Till Rover jumped the big high fence and bowled the daft cat over.
   Mullarkey licked his wounds and thought, 'It's lucky I'm alive.
   This morning I had six lives left, but now it's only.... '

5. Mullarkey found a tub of cream, delicious, white and thick,
   He ate so much it made him ill, he'd never felt so sick.
   Mullarkey groaned and held his tum and rolled upon the floor.
   This morning he had five lives left, but now it's only…

6. Mullarkey climbed a tree to catch a sparrow on a twig,
   But little branches in the air aren't made for cats so big.
   'I want to fly!' Mullarkey cried while falling from the tree.
   This morning he had four lives left, but now it's only…

7. Mullarkey came in from the cold and stretched out by the fire,
   He fell asleep and never saw the flames grow higher and higher.
   He dreamed he was a sizzling steak, and woke to find it true!
   This morning he had three lives left, but now it's only…

8. Mullarkey found a cardboard box, a super place to sleep in,
   Then someone came and picked it up and dropped it in the dustbin!
   Mullarkey meowed, 'Please let me out! Where's everybody gone?
   This morning I had two lives left, but now it's only…'

- Poor Mullarkey! Didn't he get into lots of trouble? Do you think they were all accidents, or were some of them his own fault? Let's listen again and see which were just accidents he couldn't help, and which happened because he was doing something silly.

  Read the verses again, stopping after each one to ask the children if it was Mullarkey's own fault when he lost a life. Mostly it was!

  Do children have nine lives like cats? No. That means we have to be extra careful. What happened to Mullarkey when he stepped into the road without looking? What might happen to us if we cross the road without looking? Can we just cross our fingers and hope we shall be all right?

- Teach the song, explaining the words and using it to reinforce the message that there are all sorts of dangers in the world and that we can't trust to luck to keep us out of trouble.

  As an alternative, use the song 'Life Is a Beautiful Thing', which talks about us not having nine lives like a cat.

BIBLE BACKGROUND

Good sense will protect you.
Understanding will guard you.
Solomon in Proverbs 2:11

YOU'LL GET BURNT IF YOU PLAY WITH FIRE

MATERIAL FOR PHOTOCOPYING

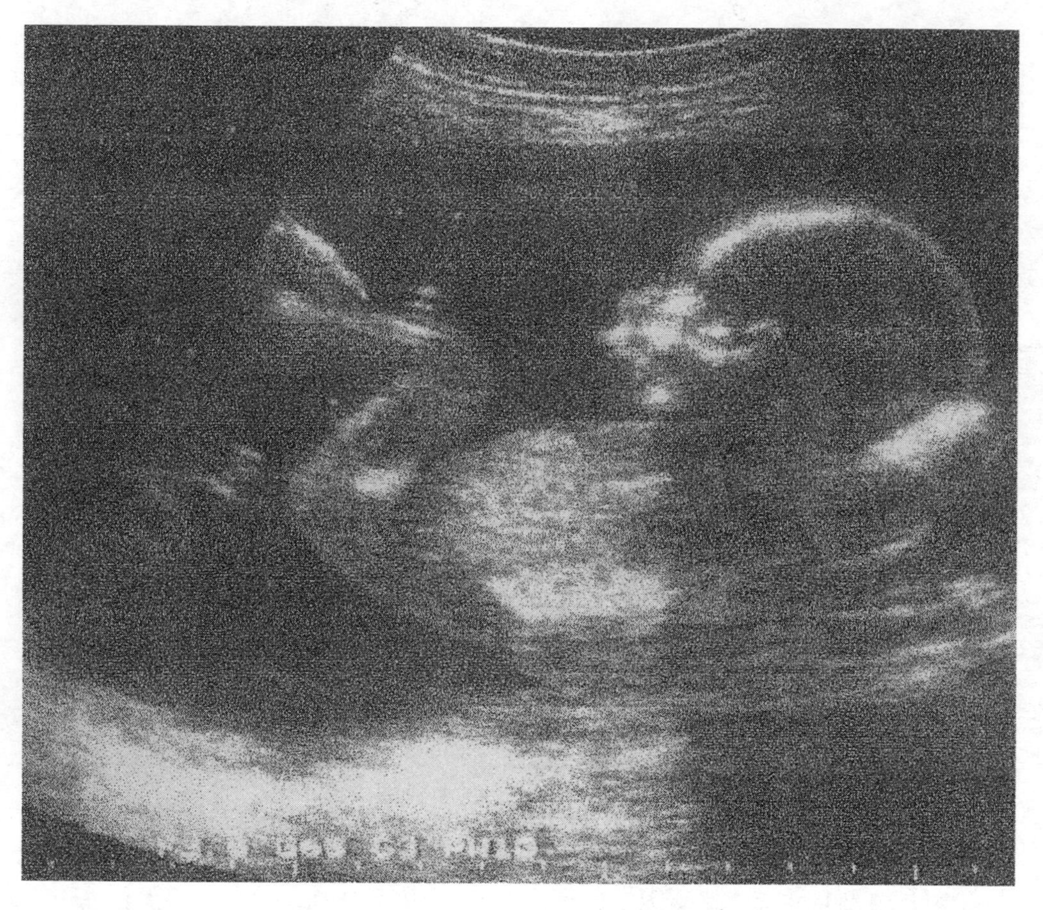

Ultrasound scan of an unborn baby

Jesus — happy

Jesus — frowning

Jesus — crying

Jesus — caring

Jesus — angry

Simon — angry

Simon — frowning

Woman — tearful

Woman — happy

Child — frightened

INDEX TO THEMES

INDEX TO BIBLE REFERENCES

OLD TESTAMENT

NEW TESTAMENT